.2

To Ellyana —

The gate is now wide open!

August 13, 2022

Brandon!

The Sunset Stallion

and the Curse of the Camel

173 poems that rhyme

by
Byron von Rosenberg

2

The Sunset Stallion and the Curse of the Camel

Cover design by Heather von Rosenberg

Interior design by Sharon von Rosenberg

Back cover photo by Erin von Rosenberg

Published by Red Mountain Creations

P.O. Box 172

High Ridge, MO 63049

www.idontwanttokissallama.com

redmountain@swbell.net

1-866-SEA-GULS

Publisher's Cataloging-in-Publication Data

provided by Five Rainbows Cataloging Services

Names: von Rosenberg, Byron, author. |

von Rosenberg, Heather, illustrator. https://www.facebook.com/zulterithcreations/

zulterithcreations@gmail.com

Title: The sunset stallion and the curse of the camel: 173 poems that rhyme /

Byron von Rosenberg; [illustrated by] Heather von Rosenberg.

Description: Byrnes Mill, MO: Red Mountain Creations, 2017.

Identifiers: ISBN 978-0-9910804-4-1 (hardcover)

Subjects: LCSH: American poetry. | Humorous poetry. |

Grief--Poetry. | Imagination--Poetry. |

BISAC: POETRY / American / General. |

POETRY / Subjects & Themes / Death, Grief, Loss. |

HUMOR / Form / Limericks & Verse.

Classification: LCC PS3622.O57 S86 2017 (print) | LCC PS3622.O57

(ebook) | DDC 811/.6--dc23.

Printed in the United States of America by Bang Printing of Brainerd, MN.

The Sunset Stallion
and the Curse of the Camel

**is dedicated to
Sharon, Ryan and Erin
von Rosenberg**

who unlatched the gate . . .

An alphabetical list of poems begins on page 142.

THE SUNSET STALLION

The broken horse would never
test the paddock gate
for it would surely fear
an undirected fate.
The bridle and the saddle
are the only world it knows
and guided by the fence
round and round it goes.
I have never seen it
lift its head to look
nor shown inclination
to cross the shallow brook.
It never would have wondered
how it felt to race the wind
nor e'er aspired to be
imagination's friend.
Slow and sure the easy path
to shelter and its feed,
its spirit's insignificant
and easy to concede.
And so I left the gate unlatched
just by happenstance
unconcerned the plodding horse
would dare to take the chance.
But there! The open gate
tells me I was wrong.
A stallion in the sunset
gallops – bold and strong!
Nostrils flared and ears laid back
it scarcely touches ground.
Freedom it desired
and freedom it has found!
The gate is now wide open
to nevermore be closed.

The stallion craved that freedom
more than I supposed.
And as I watch I wonder
if I let my fancy run
if it would pass the racing horse
and catch the setting sun.

Inspiration is all around us!

I was invited to recite my poems for the third graders
at Blevins Elementary School in Eureka, Missouri in 2010
and have done so each year since then. In 2014 I compared
reading a story to riding a horse in a ring and
writing your own work to racing across the prairie.
Two girls suggested I write a poem with that theme
and "The Sunset Stallion" is the result.

On the next page, "Curse of the Camel" was inspired by
the guests, goats and camels at Grant's Farm in St. Louis
and by my wife Sharon's mother's unique way of waking
her in time for school once as a teenager.

And "Weight is Stable", which follows it, is from a comment
made by my mother's doctor at a visit she made
in October of 2016.

There is always something to write about.
You just have to listen . . .

CURSE OF THE CAMEL

I had a dream this morning
attacked by hungry goats
which led me to write this,
one of my oddest anecdotes.
They were munching on my clothes
as goats all tend to do
when one of them began
to talk instead of chew.
"What 'cha doin' here?"
it asked in Rural-ese.
"Don't 'cha know we bite
and you could catch our fleas?
This here is a dream
so I'll turn into a camel!"
and right away it grew a hump
and spat just like that mammal!
I shook my head and wiped my face
and hollered, "Go away!"
but the camel said, "Not a chance!
You have school today!"
"What an awful nightmare!"
I grumbled and I groaned.
"Worse if you don't get up now!"
the camel then intoned.
I was so confused
I opened up my eyes
and standing there was – My Mom! -
much to my surprise,
and in her hand a bucket,
a lunch bag and my books
and on her face the worst I've seen
of her "You're in trouble!" looks.
So I struggled to my feet
and put my clothes on - Quick!

I didn't tell my mom
but I really did feel sick.

SHE TURNED INTO . . .

A CAMEL!

What an awful curse!
But I had to go to school
and that's a whole lot worse!

One of my favorites.
Mom doesn't like that I turned her into a camel, however. . .

WEIGHT IS STABLE

I think my doctor thinks
I eat like horses at a table
But does he mean one or all of them
When he says my weight is "stable"?

A POOR POET'S ADVICE

Study. Practice. Read.
If you're going to be a writer
there are several things you'll need.
Grow imagination.
What's it like to be a bird?
Listen to your grandma.
There is wisdom in each word.
Learn vocabulary.
Know each grammar rule
and don't forget to have some fun
even while at school.
Take a walk on sunny days
and sometimes in the rain.
Let your mind explore
things you can't explain.
Watch for inspiration
and catch it when it comes.
Find it in the whispering wind
or the beat of distant drums.
Write when you're inspired
and write when you are not.
If you want to be a writer
you have to write a lot!
Find a place that's special
and likewise time to spend
so writing is as natural
as meeting an old friend.
Find someone you can read to
who loves you just enough
to tell you when your story's good
and when it's kind of rough.
When you get a chance
read it to a crowd.
There's nothing like an author
who dares to read out loud.
Do you remember taking books
to your mom when you were three?

Loving books and writing them
sets ideas free.
And while it might be nice to have
money, fame and glory
the greatest joy a writer gets
is discovering a story.

When asked a question, I find my best answers in a poem. The preceding poem
is my answer to the question, "What should I do to become a writer?"

I AM THE WIND

When branches bend
on windless day
I wonder what
could make them sway
and looking I
spy in the tree
a squirrel looking
back at me.
I laugh to think
that one so small
could make a tree
to move at all.
And then I think
of cosmos grand
and the power of
my tiny hand.
The squirrel laughs
and jumps again
and creates for me
a thought just then:

'Tis life that makes the branches bend
and sometimes more than does the wind.

THE OLD WAR HORSE

The old war horse
hears the trumpet call
and once again he gathers
his strength to give his all.
He is alone aware
of the courage war requires
and despite its depth he knows
that he more quickly tires.
The younger horses watch
wondrous and blasé
thinking that the battle
is nothing more than play.
They don't yet fear the sound
of cannon fire and gun
or know that death can catch them
however fast they run.
"Nothing wrong with that,"
the war horse seems to think
for youth is an elixir
one has but once to drink.
He likes to stand beside them
for they are strong and brave
yet luck and circumstance will more
determine barn or grave.
The flags are all unfurled
and the battle lines are drawn.
The war horse feels the whip
and hurtles towards the dawn.
Farther now and faster
at the rising sun he races
stronger for the conquering
of every fear he faces.
And there are some who say
the war horse conquered death
for it was courage he inhaled
with each and every breath.

SUDDENLY AN OWL

Suddenly an owl
flashed before my eyes
and from my reverie
I awakened in surprise.
For the owl was so far away
and quiet in its tree
and I wonder why an owl
would fix its sights on me.
Is stimulus its goal
or am I simply prey?
An owl suddenly
made me think today.
For silently then suddenly
changes do occur
with lives and places never
to be the way they were.
For such an unexpected thing
how can I be ready?
Only through my character
holding strong and steady.
Suddenly an owl
and no time at all to blink
yet should it come tomorrow
I'll be more prepared, I think.

Life can change quickly and with little notice.
A change in employment at age 58 and related experiences
led to these two poems.

QUICKLY FOR QUICKLY

When trials were tough
and answers were few
in spite of myself
that's when I grew.
And losing one time
meant winning the next
for life does not follow
a writ-in-stone text.
I made my choices
and make more today.
You do the same
and find your own way.
It might break your heart
to be chasing a star
but do it you must
to know who you are.
Oh! How I wish
that by clearing the field
those answers you seek
could be quickly revealed.
But all I can do
is to say with a sigh
that I've done my best
and it's your turn to try.
I wish there were more
I could say that I've learned
but the deepest of wisdom
has to be earned.
When you seek wisdom
you'll find tribulation
for it is through trial
there comes revelation.
Yet when other men fail
you will stand tall
and see for a moment
over the wall.
Remember that moment
and share it in word –

Quickly! – for quickly
wisdom is blurred.
And in that one instant
e'er it passes from sight
share what you see
of grace, truth and light!

TWO RAINBOWS

Two rainbows parallel,
A grand and wondrous sight,
Different but together,
One soft, the other bright.
Two rainbows, every color,
Beauty unsurpassed,
Like two hearts reaching out
To find true love at last.
Two rainbows flowing full
In sparkling summer air,
A treasure for the eyes
And like our love, so rare.
Two rainbows individual
Yet everywhere they touch,
Blending into one.
Dear, I love you so much!
Two rainbows stretching up
Following the rain,
Long after all the storms have passed
Our love will yet remain.
A heaven for each other
You and I shall be
Remembered and reminded by
Each rainbow that we see.

LAST CALL OF THE BUGLER

Soft short notes
the splendors of breath
that hold for a moment
the advent of death,
and somehow the melody
hangs on the breeze
while the lips and the lungs
that played it with ease
struggle against
their weakness of form
wherein beats a heart
gentle and warm.
Soft, short and sweet
yet courageous and brave
these are testament tones
to the love that he gave.
The last note is longer
and as I strain so to hear
thousands of stars
in the sunset appear.
Each light is a life
the music has found
- The bugler reborn! -
for each raises the sound
of the triumph
of the spirit of man
living forever
as no body yet can.
Listen with me
to the bugler's last call;
raise yours to your lips
as he lets his fall.

Written for my brother Gene on a plane as I went to visit him one last time.
He was bugler in our Scout troop and my book, *The Toy Bugle*, is dedicated to him.

BECAUSE IT MOVES

I have planned my life
to glide in gentle grooves
but find to my dismay
it like an earthquake moves.
Structures I thought sturdy –
family, friends, finances –
now in ruins lie.
What are survival's chances?
Because it moves it is
a story never–ending.
Life is moving forward
and deliberate defending.
What items do you cherish most?
What values have you chosen?
Do the seasons change them
or are they forever frozen?
If there were one thing only
to pass on to our youth
I'd select this adage –
to always seek the truth.
Deliberately and doggedly
or via inspiration,
in every life the truth
will be a firm foundation.
Because it moves success
will change with tide and time
yet those who practice honesty
will find a peace sublime.

There was an earthquake in Italy on the same day
as I lost medical insurance in 2016.

THE BEST OF THE MAGICIAN

Distraction. Deception.
Look the other way.
He practiced and he used these
every single day.
He knew it wasn't right
to offer such a lie.
He was just a poor magician
who barely could get by.
He focused on his audience
as he never had before
hoping that in memories
there'd be some kind of cure.
And if he ever speaks
of the day the curtain fell
you'll touch the best of heaven
and brush the worst of hell.
For on that final day
when the crowd was down to two
he performed the hardest task
that he would ever do.
He simply disappeared
before the final act
and in so doing did reveal
how much he loved yet lacked.
"The visions I can conjure
of good times long ago
cannot cure your cancer
as both of us now know.
We have fooled ourselves
and smiled in spite of pain
and we have seen the sun
that shines above the rain.
We have soared as eagles
for we gave our spirits wings
but I must now to earth
and you to higher things.
I give to you the wand of love

I used to cast the spell.
Let me kiss you one last time."
Then from the sky he fell.
And you may see him wander
through the marketplace sometime
rejected for his failures.
He does not own a dime.
Yet they say some magic lingers
of the failed magician's best
who in spite of all his failures
will tell you he is blessed.

ASHES IN THE MORNING

Ashes in the morning
from flames that climbed much higher
are all that now remains
of that once glorious fire.
A gentle breath to stir them
yet all the heat is gone
and there is no flame rising
today to beckon the dawn.
But now a hand to lift them
and another touch of air
and there's suddenly reward
with one ember's minuscule flare.
Kindling laid down softly
to catch that single spark
and soon there is a fire
daring to challenge the dark.
Ashes in the morning
were all that had remained
and yet with love and confidence
the light has been regained.

A LITTLE BOY'S VIEW OF ETERNITY

As a little boy in church
I heard "eternity"
and wondered would that giant word
e'er apply to me.
I pondered in the car
on the way back home
and barefoot in the creek
when I had time to roam.
I listened to the stories
that the old men tell
yet still could not understand
eternity very well.
It was finally time for me
to start to go to school
and as I did my musing
got a brand new tank of fuel.
"We are going shopping," said my Mom,
"for a whole new set of clothes
'cause I'd just die to see you
go to school in those."
I'm still not sure what happened
when we got into the store
but I no longer wonder
about eternity any more
'cause before I turned around
my Saturday was gone
and eternity began
when Mom said, "Try this on!"

My Mom mentioned that as a little girl she wondered what eternity meant.
I offered her this understanding I achieved as a little boy.

IVAN THE TERRIER
ROLLS IN DIRT

Ivan the Terrier likes to roll
in the dirt and dust
not for any reason
other than he must.
I can give him baths
and wash the mud away
but Ivan puts it right back on
when he goes out to play.
And so I watch and wonder
as dust clouds swirl and rise
if there's something Ivan
helps me realize.
He hasn't asked for anything.
He's happy on his own,
free of cares and worries
into which I've grown.
Ivan knows instinctively
what I did as a boy:
It is in the simplest things
we find the greatest joy!

Ivan taught me many lessons. More later . . .

ETERNITY FOR AN OLD MAN

It's a moment that gets longer
even as it nears
'cause the bathroom's always further
than it first appears.

Written immediately after the "Little Boy's View"!

DANGER IS THE POET

Poverty for a poet
is the source of all his riches
for his ragged raiment reminds him
to notice holes and stitches.
The things that tear apart
and those that hold together
and what will be his fate
with the changing of the weather –
wealth for these is easy fix
so no one contemplates
lest he has been inside the house
and now shivers at the gates.
His curse is also blessing
whose teeth chatter in the wind
and knows for his proximity
where human lives must end.
He treasures very deeply
the one who comfort offers
and empties for the same
the tidbits of his coffers.

Everything is taken
that from the truth would blind him
so his words can flow unfettered
for there is naught to bind him.

Danger is the poet
with nothing left to lose
who walks the tortured path
not even he would choose.

THE TRAGEDY OF WILLIAM TELL

The tragedy
of William Tell
is though he aimed
and shot so well
that someone made him
risk his son
and though on that
one day he won
he wasn't made
a knight or king
to see that such
an awful thing
would not happen
e'er again
to him or to
the least of men.
And when your hand
is forced that way
I hope you're able,
can and may
resist the notion
you must choose
between two different
ways to lose
and find a way
to win the game
so no one has to
face the same:

the agony, the woe, the curse
of deciding what is wrong or worse.

THE ENGLISH SOLUTION

A cultural phenomenon
that all can plainly see
is the Englishman solves everything
when he sits down for tea.
Is the weather cold?
Is it instead too hot?
It simply doesn't matter.
Sit down and share a pot!
Are you situated
in Timbuktu or Rome?
Have a cup of tea
and pretend that you're at home.
Are you nodding off
or sitting down to read?
In either case a cup of tea
is exactly what you need.
It is quite peculiar
but perhaps it is a way
to put aside the problems
that face you twice a day
and ponder on the things that make
the universe align.
I suppose for that
a cup of tea's just fine.

Dedicated to my daughter-in-law Heather
and to her parents, Phil and Rose Parrott
of Leicester, England. Go Foxes!

THE SPIDER WEB DILEMMA

Should I spoil the spider web
to view the pristine creek
or is its beauty intricate
the wonder that I seek?
Is it a distraction
to simply brush away
so I can reach my goal
as planned without delay?
And as I pause I wonder
why I hesitate.
When was the last time anyone
pondered on my fate?
And have I been concerned
with my fellow man
or focused far too much
and only on my plan?
Is there a way ahead
that preserves both plan and web?
I search for an alternative
as the sunlight starts to ebb.
And though the web may last
for only one more hour
I have come to understand
how grace must blend with power.

This poem was inspired by a Facebook post
from my friend Al Gross.

DON QUIXOTE'S GHOST

Perhaps I have been haunted
by Don Quixote's ghost
as from all the literature
I resemble him the most.
For I understand a windmill
indeed can be a giant
whereby the whimsical
are crushed and made compliant.
Everything I say and do
is captured on this phone
and since it asks the questions
my thoughts aren't mine alone.
For I am so dependent
on technology
that I wonder if my wondering
is more it then me.
And thus I set out on a walk
with my gadgets left behind.
What an oddball notion:
To see better when I'm blind!
Will they laugh at me?
I choose to take that chance!
Don Quixote rides again
with a pencil as my lance.

WITH MY WINGS

They tell me it is folly
To fly with my own wings
And that it would be better
To stick to earthly things.
But I persist in foolishness
Each and every day
Steadfast in the knowledge
That this is wisdom's way.
I speak my words to many
But my followers are few
And yet the fountain overflows

With thoughts both bold and true.
There is no water standing
To be poisoned dark with hate
For love alone that inundates
Can alter mankind's fate.
A future that was dark and bleak
Now sparkles in the light
And those who thought that love was weak
Marvel at its might.
With my wings that were so frail
I fly above and see
That when I dare to dream my soul
Soars forever free.

ELOQUENCE BEYOND

Sometimes in the awkwardness
of human speech is found
lovingkindness eloquent
more than any sound.
It isn't in a word
as much is in a deed.
The awkwardness is something
all of us should heed.
Listen to the ones you love
as love pours back on you
more than what was given!
That's how you know it's true.
And when the ears no longer hear
and the tongue does not obey
it is love and love alone
'twill have the final say.
Eloquence beyond
the awkwardness of speech
practiced for a lifetime
does through example teach.

For our daughter, Erin, who consistently inspires!

FIRST GRADE SILHOUETTE

A silhouette a child once drew
in his first grade class
fades but only slightly
as the decades pass.
The man who was the boy
pauses for a glance
wondering what might have been
with just another chance.
The silhouette is silent
and offers not a clue
for the past grants not redemption
for the deeds we never do.
"It's just a silhouette,"
I excuse myself
and bury it with papers
on the basement shelf.
Who was the lad who greeted
each new day with joy?
In the man does there yet live
a trace of that lost boy?
Or is it rather that the man
and not the boy is lost
whose ambitious dreams
on failure's heap were tossed?
"But a dream I lost is still a dream
should I not forget,"
says the man who was the boy
who drew the silhouette.

The silhouette is still on the shelf somewhere
in the basement . . .

HOT CHOCOLATE IN A COFFEE CUP

Hot chocolate in a coffee cup
is pleasantly surprising
which causes me to contemplate
and think about revising
my evaluation of
the trail of life I've led
perhaps to be less critical
and more positive instead.
I suffer much for my art
or at least I think I do
but chocolate in my coffee cup
makes me wonder if that's true.
Isn't it amazing
that something sweet and nice
can change my attitude
more than sage advice?
For suddenly I see that things
I say I can't abide
help me find the truth that once
was hidden deep inside.
Sweet surprising chocolate
makes me sit straight up
and wonder what tomorrow
will put inside my cup.

Most of my signings are done at the Storybook Sweets store
at Grant's Farm. Perhaps this is a consistent theme . . .

VISIONS OF A PLOW HORSE

What does the plow horse see
beyond the farthest row?
If it were set free
how far would it go?
My vision of the plow horse
is from behind the plow
the only view the rulers
of this world allow.
But the plow horse lifts its head
on an odd occasion
and as I follow too my mind
is subject to invasion.
Thoughts it never harbored
now set sail through me.
Beyond this patch of earth
they travel far and free
across, above the fence posts
to the ground you till
calling to you gently
but never holding still.
Yet if they should lift your gaze
to the sun and sky,
if they should cause you wonder
not just how but why,
then perhaps the vision
of a plow horse and a man
more than random musings
unveil a greater plan,
one that spans the chasms
of distance and of year
bonding us together
with that we hold most dear.
Love of land and liberty
in which the spirit grows,
I see a different plow horse
as it completes its rows.
Blessings like the rain
are given, never earned,
which from a humble plow horse
lately I have learned.

THE CHANGING PIECE
OF THE PUZZLE

I am the changing piece
trying to fit in.
There is no longer place for me
whence I did begin.
It is a lonely journey
for rarely do I touch
much less interlock with those
whom I love so much.
For I seek less a place to light
than to see the puzzle whole
confusing those who comprehend
a more specific goal.
I must be apart
though ofttimes I would stay.
The changing piece can never
long lodge in the array.
It looks afar to see
how its world arranges.
With time and wisdom gained
it can predict the changes.
And as its edges fray
it may see a spot appear
and find a home again
as its journey's end draws near.

Inspired by a cloud that seemed to "fit" into the one next to it
. . . and then it didn't.

GRINS FOR ALPACAS

Smiles for llamas
and grins for alpacas
break out in New York,
Beijing and Caracas.
And though we might answer
to different kings
the people who matter
agree on such things.
A stroll in the park,
a day at the zoo,
in searching for peace
these each can be clue.
Find a connection
on which to agree
and a whole new perspective
is easy to see.
Sure, there are reasons
we don't get along
but liking alpacas
and llamas ain't wrong.
And though this world never
will be of one mind
if you seek common ground
that's what you'll find.

SAID THE EAGLE TO THE MOLE

"Why don't you come fly with me?"
said the eagle to the mole
who in reply dug deeper
and huddled in its hole.
"Think of all the things you'd see
and the places you would go!"

But deeper went the mole,
its answer clearly, "No!"
"We can go to dinner
with my whole family!"
But even in the dark
the mole could plainly see
what were the intentions
that the eagle meant for it.
It would not negotiate
or compromise one bit.
It meant being stubborn
and thought to be a fool
which is not the same as being one
as a general rule.

CUCUMBERSOME

There's a little town, they say,
On Missouri's plains
Where cucumbers proliferate
Instead of wheatly grains.
They send them out in truckloads,
On boxcars if by rail,
And if you call the city hall
They'll send one FREE by mail!
They have recipes and cookbooks
At the general store
And no matter what the season,
Cucumbers galore!
But should you ever go there
Take this advice from me:
You'd better lock your car
Or that's where they'll all be!

THE DACHSHUND'S REACH

I could not believe
until I just saw
how a dachshund can reach
its ear with its paw.
Its leg is so short
and body so long!
For scratching its ears
a dachshund's all wrong.
But with a contortion
and incredible strain
the dachshund makes happen
what should be in vain.
"Scratching my ear?
Yes it can be done!
Impossible odds
make victory fun!"

CHUCK THE DACHSHUND MEETS A MOLE

Chuck the Dachshund met a mole
When he stuck his head down in its hole
But from the frantic sounds I heard
It wasn't friendship he incurred.
Now Chuckie is a stubborn pup
From the mounds of dirt that he dug up.
Determination is his thing!
He chased the moles throughout the spring.
Whenever they came up for air
They'd find Chuck the Dachshund guarding there.
Chuckie never had a doubt
That he would one day chase them out.
They left beneath a summer sky

Never wishing him, "Good-bye!"
Chuckie didn't miss them much
But the yard is different for his touch.
It seems the obstinance he had
Tore the ground up pretty bad!
That same persistence I must show
If I ever want the grass to grow
Since for the dog and all those moles
My pristine lawn's just clumps and holes!

HIS MAJESTY'S FIRETRUCK

They say the King of England
drove a fire truck
and might have been a fireman
if he'd had better luck.
Instead he had to sit
through endless social teas
and give up his dreams
to issue droll decrees.
He'd sneak out of the palace
and to the local station
where he'd get to drive a truck
instead of lead a nation.
And I hope it gave him happiness
and joy deep in his soul
to imagine for a moment
he could live a different role.
And I think I know the feeling!
My reports are overdue.
Both cars need repair
and the dollars are too few.
So I guess I'm pretty glad
imagination's free
and that a mighty king can feel
a little bit like me.

ENOUGH IT IS

It should come
as no surprise
that Shakespeare's past
is all surmise.
Storyteller
grand was he
so much more
than history.
So ponder not
his daily toil
lest ye mystery
despoil.
Enough it is
he lived and wrote
and for his vision
rightly smote
the dragons of
the titled clan
for born he was
not nobleman.
Imagination,
effort, skill,
with such he ventured
as I will
and for my taking
of the dare
learn I will
what heart can bear.
For poet has
no resting place
save the Muses
him embrace.
And for that closure
all I give.
I live to write
and write to live.

NOT BY TRANSACTION

I wonder at the stunts
and ruses we pull
just trying to live
like regular people
'cause you gotta have money
to live on this earth
yet comprehend quickly
that's not all that life's worth.
So how does one balance
the tricks of the trade
with the value of friendships
honestly made?
In physics there's always
an equal reaction
but one cannot build trust
just by transaction.
And even if so
that's no way to live!
The way to get more
than you want is to give.
Love is a treasure
with which you can't pay.
It doesn't buy anything!
You give it away.
And when you have none
look back on the shelf.
By giving not taking
you made it yourself.
I don't understand
why people don't try
to give away love
when they sell or they buy.
For all man's achievement
he still will be cursed
if he cannot find ways
to put someone else first.

THE HORSE
WITH THE DISAPPEARING TAIL

I saw a giant white stallion
as my dreams began to clear
and much to my startled surprise
I watched his tail disappear!
I thought it very odd
for a horse with no tail is so strange
and what today is most certain
is most certainly soon going to change.
A tail is a horse's friend
and honor and loyalty mine
and the horse without a tail
is for modern times a sure sign.
Promises made long ago
mean nothing at all in this age
but it's never okay to tell lies
and simply say, "I disengage."
"A horse should have a tail
and promises made should be kept,"
the horse without a tail
told me last night as I slept.

INSIDE PASSAGE

Soft and silent waves
lift mists up towards the sky
which the hidden eagle
pierces with its cry.
Alone, adrift and lost
I paddle aimlessly
as I try to reach
my unknown destiny.
There are many times
that I have seen the land
but I tarry long in waters
as I try to understand.
For no one else has witnessed
the world as I have seen,

wonders that the fog of life
is so quick to screen.
For – lo! – the inside passage
brightens far ahead
and it is by such glimmers
of hope that I am led.
Softly, slowly, smoothly,
I leave no lasting trace
and yet the inside passage
has touched me with its grace.
And I hope much as the light
guides me on my way
that I might do the same
for someone else today.

SPEAKING IS STEEL

They say that being quiet
is a good thing for the soul
and helps in understanding
one's designated role.
And I who have long listened
to sayings such as these
understand the pleasure
of listening to the breeze.
And yet the comprehension
that quietly I seek
forces me to rise
and courageously to speak.
For in my contemplations
the truth is strong and real
and if silence is golden
then speaking must be steel.

I worked so hard to keep quiet in my job
and now work harder still to be heard through my poems.
As Sharon says, "Go figure!"

A PIECE OF DRIFTWOOD

I'm a piece of driftwood
Floating on the sea.
There's not much of anything
Matters much to me.
Someday I may land
On a distant shore
Where I'll find the world
No different than before.
I am tossed about
By waves so great and strong
That this little piece of driftwood
May not last for long.
People look at me
And say that it's a shame
Not ever recognizing
That they are just the same.
They have so little time
To cause the world to change
And why they even want to
To driftwood seems so strange.
They are not much bigger
On the ocean than am I
But they disturb their drifting
By always asking, "Why?"
"Why am I not able
To choose my destiny?"
"Why am I tossed about
Like driftwood on the sea?"
Why should a piece of driftwood
Bother with such things?
I'll just wait and see
What tomorrow brings.
It may or may not change me
As on the sea I dance.
A driftwood knows its fate
Is merely circumstance.
There's a certain calmness
When I recognize
That driftwood floats upside down.
Who cares if I capsize?
Storms that swirl around me
Always keep me spinning

But tomorrow is another day
To make a new beginning.
Not why but where the question
That I wonder now
And once that one is answered
What remains is, "How?"
For it is the fate of driftwood
Constantly to roam.
As a piece of driftwood
The journey is my home.
And tomorrow is another day
That home is where I'll be,
A tiny piece of driftwood
Atop a giant sea.

POETRY PURE

I treasure the times
my feet lead the tour
for a walk in the woods
is poetry pure
with sunlight that filters
through the tops of the trees
that ever so gently
rock with the breeze.
The call of the geese
and the nightingale's song
propose to my spirit,
"Come! Follow along!"
And suddenly I
am one with the whole
for poetry pure
has rescued my soul.
It watches in wonder
as the golden leaves fall
and rides on the winds
as it answers their call.

NEW ZEBRA IN BALTIMORE

It was too tall and too skinny and so badly misshaped
But the label said, "ZEBRA" so when it escaped
As it so often did, time, time and again
They'd catch it and put it back in the same pen.
"That's not a zebra!" a little girl cried.
"It's got a long neck and spots and it's too tall to hide
Behind rocks or bushes or even a tree.
It's a giraffe and that really should be easy to see."
It caused consternation in Baltimore's zoo
And they committeed like monkeys to decide what to do.
And though it was clear that its neck was too long
They never admitted that they had been wrong.
They moved the giraffe as a concession to sense
To where it could no longer step over the fence.
The other giraffes accepted it well
And it was content as near as can tell.
The point of this story is that they'll label YOUR crate
And try to decide for you what is your fate.
And here is a question to perplex your cerebra:
Can you be a giraffe if you're seen as a zebra?
They did it to me but I didn't then know
As a baby giraffe how tall that I'd grow.
But I'm now sure who I am in my own cerebellum
And when they call me a zebra I'm quite quick to tell 'em
That labelling me so just makes me laugh
'cause though I like zebras I am a giraffe.
Yes, they tagged me a zebra and I didn't agree
And when that happens to you, who will you be?

I had a dream and saw the giraffe picture from
my llama book with the caption that is now
the title to this poem. It was only a dream
so if you live in Baltimore, please don't take offence!

A HAT ON A POST
ON A SUMMER'S DAY

I saw a hat that rested
Atop the rugged post
And wondered of the person
Who before had been its host.
Did they leave it here on purpose
Or did they just forget?
Did they fill their life with meaning
Or tinge it with regret?
I think of all the hours
I've spent to earn my bread
And how I might have made them
Significant instead.
It's silly how a hat
Can make me think this way
As it sits atop a post
On this summer's day.
But then again it's stranger
To simply walk on past
Not pondering the life
That is slipping by so fast.
And so I take a moment
As I so often do
To write down what I'm thinking
And offer it to you.

I wrote this poem on a hot and humid day
when I was doing a book signing at Grant's Farm in front
of the General's Store.

HARRY THE HAMSTER

Harry the Hamster
loved to eat cake
and scheduled a picnic
down by the lake.
Cheesecake was spread
and guests were invited
but it wasn't long
e'er chickens were sighted.
They gathered and clucked
and ate all the cake!
Then Harry the Hamster
started to shake.
"He's crazed about chickens
uninvited and rude
who don't even bother
to thank him for food!"
So let us give thanks
for this our next meal,
glad Harry the Hamster
is not really real.

EBULLIENT OR EBULLIENT

Ebullient has two meanings.
One's exuberant
which is what I called my wife
and that is what I meant.
The other one is boiling
or greatly agitated.
If at all the meanings
are distantly related.
I didn't know the second one
but it's the one she read
and I wish I had selected
another word instead.
For now she is ebullient
like meaning number two.

Oh! Woe is me for thinking
how well the words I knew!
The bullion is ebullient
I left heating on the stove.
It's a meaning I'll remember
ebulliently, by Jove!
Not knowing all the meanings
made me seem a fool
and I think it's sometimes best
that we let silence rule.

GUILTY AT THE MALL

The mall cops must think that I'm
Guilty of a crime
Because they watch and follow me
Almost all the time.
But I'm a model citizen!
I get straight A's at school.
I think it was in second grade
That I last broke a rule.
But now they say I talk too loud!
I'm disturbing other folks.
But the reason they don't like me is
They're the butt of all my jokes.
I said they did an MRI
On a cop down at the mall
But couldn't tell if he had half a brain
Or rather none at all.
It made me really popular
With the crowd in which I run
And glad that mall cops aren't allowed
To have or use a gun!

Thanks to Mia and friends at a local mall.

JASPER'S COUNTRY

Jasper the Llama looks a bit crazed
But if you knew what he thought you might be amazed.
The faraway look in his eyes that you see
Is the birth of a yearning in his heart to be free.
He knows there's a place on a faraway hill
Where llamas are free to roam as they will.
And though he is good and does what he's told
The desire in his heart takes him far from the fold.

"There's a river that flows
Clean, clear and cold
Deep in the valley
Of the free and the bold!
The flowers and grasses
That grow in that place
Belong to the llama
That dares run the race.
My heart sees the target
But I walk with my feet.
Until I arrive
What and how will I eat?"

It's questions like that which give Jasper pause
But I know that one day he'll set out for his cause.
And high on a mountain past fear and regret
I'll see standing tall his proud silhouette.

For the look in his eyes
Is the same that I see
In the ones from the mirror
That look back at me.

In honor of Annie the Llama at Grant's Farm.

LAST YEAR MONKEYS
THIS YEAR COWS

Last year she liked monkeys! She said they were cool.
She had ten in her room and five in the pool.
I bought a gorilla, baboon, chimpanzee
And capuchin she said looked a whole lot like me!
Gibbons and lemurs! Primates, every kind!
I lost half of my wallet and most of my mind.
Then somehow she made them each and all disappear!
She says she likes cows better this year.
I'm learning about them as fast as I can
But I realize now I don't know the plan.
Is next year vicunas, alpacas, or llamas?
Do you prefer sleeping in a gown or pajamas?
Do you like music from violin or guitar?
Decisions like that decide who you are.
Everyone has a part deep inside
That acts as a compass, a map or a guide.
Young people grow. They need room to roam
And also a reason to find their way home.

Last year a monkey.

This year a cow.

Isn't it grand that love does allow
For changes of favorites in all kinds of things?
And I'll get her a cow for the joy that it brings.

From a comment made by a customer at the
I Don't Want to Kiss a Llama! store when it was in Chesterfield Mall.

POPCORN WITH AN ARTIST

I ate some popcorn late last night
With an artist I once knew.
We talked about our lives
And, through them, how we grew.
Joy and celebration!
Tragedy and tears!
Satisfaction greater
than money, fame or cheers.
I like mine with butter.
She said that she did not.
Either way we like it
Fresh and piping hot.
I renewed connection
From days so long ago
And found a depth of soul
That before I did not know.
The sketches and the paintings
That I did not understand
Make sense because I know
The heart behind the hand.
A little bit of popcorn,
A smile, a nod, a wink,
Might make a better world
For you and I, I think.

RECUERDO LA SEÑORA

Señora de la Vega
Taught with song and dance
And Spanish was like magic
So much did it entrance.
I remember counting,
"Uno, dos, y tres,"
And how I could, in language,
Find new ways to express
And to explain
The world as it appeared
For a language is a blessing,
Not something to be feared.
And I hope that "La Señora"

Wherever she may be
Smiles a little bit
When she remembers me.
She sang to me a melody
That I had never heard
As I pondered on the meaning
And the wonder of each word.
And though the passing years
Make words harder to recall
When it comes to La Seňora's love
"Yo recuerdo" all.

CHAUCER'S LOT

I for one hope I am not
Fated follow Chaucer's lot.
Successful so in worldly ways
And poetry to earn high praise
And yet accused of weighty crimes
He faced feared prisons many times.
And finally with wealth secure
Plague befell that had no cure.
Yet down the road I travel now
There is likeness I'll allow.
At fiscal matters I lack skill,
Always have and likely will
For there is naught of worldly gain
That comes without its share of pain.
Robbed and robber agonize
I like Chaucer realize.
So sometimes write of stories grim,
Grieve and sometime laugh at them.
Odd how journeys intertwine!
Chaucer's fate looks much like mine.
Struggle on to earn one's bread,
Write and hope it might be read
And as the words flow from my hand
I pray that some will understand
that a story casts a lasting spell
when it has a truth to tell.

SUMMON THE MOON

There is in legend a story
That the wolf's call summons the moon
And makes me think how much smaller
The world would be less that tune.
For there is in the kingdom a question
Of consequence and of cause:
How will the world be affected
By the path I take with my paws?
For the moon may rise on its own
Without notice of mammal or man
And though naught I do may affect it
There are other things that I can.
Some of them come with the sunrise
And the opening up of the mind
While others are hidden away
And take a lifetime to find.
Am I like the wolf that howls
And imagine the moon it commands
Or is there really a power
In my mind, my heart and my hands?
Is it only an instinct
That lifts my eyes to the hill
Or is there something unique
In perseverance and will?
For like the wolf as it howls
I look beyond the black sky
Seeking out a connection
To a power greater than I.
And now at the end of my day
As my voice grows softer and weak
I may listen at last
And find the answer I seek.
It lingers like dewdrops on flowers
That shine with the light of the dawn
Bright as the sharpest of diamonds
Yet in one instant they're gone.
O! That I understood sooner
The secrets that were hidden so long!

Listen, my friend, for the answer
Before you have finished your song.
Pause for a moment and ponder
And change as the seasons now do
Then sing your song to the heavens
In hopes they will listen to you.

SHADOW OF A LEAF

I saw a shadow playing
On the trunk of that old tree
And wondered at the leaf
That I couldn't see.
And yet I saw the wind,
Invisible before.
Did the shadow of a leaf
Open up a door?
Did a thought that someone had
Many years ago
Help you understand
What you did not know?
A shadow of a leaf
On an autumn day
Tells me that when I can't see
There is yet a way.
Impossible? Impossible!
It's beyond belief
To think that I could think such things
From the shadow of a leaf.

Our daughter Erin and I used to "howl at the moon" together.
I wrote "Shadow of a Leaf" outside at Grant's Farm.

SLIPPING ON SOAP

I slipped on soap in the shower
About an hour ago.
I thought I was pretty lucky
For only stubbing one toe.
I limped to get a towel
And lifted it off of the rack
But hadn't shampooed and lathered
So I turned and hobbled right back.
I reached down to pick up the soap
Where it lay in innocent pose
But it escaped my grasp once again
And hit me right square in the nose!
I arched my back and stood up
My balance to quickly regain,
Stepped once more on the soap
And landed writhing in pain.
The soap lay still beside me
Ready to battle again
But I demurred in the knowledge
There are some battles you just cannot win.
And I wish that our politicians,
Lawyers and judges and such
Through an adventure like mine might learn
And put into practice as much.

JUST A HORSE

The farmer and the plow horse
trenched the field in May
so it could be planted
in barley, oats and hay.
"Now's the time for seeding,"
said the farmer to the horse,
"and I could use a hand,"
but it had none, of course.
All the horse could do
was shake its mane and snort
which better than a speech
was its cross retort.
"I am just a horse.

I've done the work I do
and the completion of this task
is entirely up to you."
And so I say to companies,
"You have a job. You know it!
Don't expect a business plan
because I am just a poet."

THE CLOWN
AND THE GIANT CANARY

The clown and the giant canary
Are really a very odd pair.
The canary takes the clown flying
And makes her nest right in his hair!
They draw great crowds to the circus.
People journey for hundreds of miles
But the strangest of all facts about them
Is they honor their different styles.
The clown doesn't tell the canary
It has to juggle and dance
And the canary doesn't make fun
Of the clown's very oversized pants.
When one is lacking in something
The other is quick to redeem.
They're not remotely alike
But they make a really good team.
Yet in our schools of management
They teach that you really should try
To cage the giant canary
And tell the clown he can fly!

Yes, I really did slip on the soap.
I had a dream about the clown and the giant canary.
And, no, try as I might a business plan is NOT
one of my acquired or gifted skills.

THE STRANGEST OF THINKING

The strangest of thinking
Goes on in my brain
Deep in the night
When just hours remain.
This morning I had
A very odd dream
Where creative and logic
Worked as a team.
Creative was late
And needed help getting dressed.
Logic was patient
But terribly stressed.
They got it together
And went on their way
And I hope that I find them
Later today.
It's a special occurrence
Whenever I do
For a sad fact of life
That often seems true
Is thinking creatively
Gets you in trouble
And toying with logic
Makes the dose double.
I'm tied to computers
That check on my chores
And demand that I ask
And know about yours.
With so much time spent
Typing and fretting
Creative and logic
We're mostly forgetting.
And I think we could solve
Many problems and woes
If trust were a value
That everyone chose.
Now maybe I'm wrong
But maybe I'm right
And that was my thinking
When I woke up last night.

THE HIDDEN THINGS

The squirrel looks for acorns
That it did not see fall
And yet it seems to know
Where to find them all.
My dog can find the bones
Hidden in the ground
And sometimes my day changes
With just a single sound.
Just now it was a robin
Chirping in a tree
That woke me from my daze
And set my spirit free.
And I'm amazed to find
Thoughts trapped within my mind,
Things that seem so obvious!
I wonder, "Was I blind?"
For like the squirrel with an acorn
Or the puppy with a bone
The treasure I've been searching for
Is in a place I've always known.
I only had to look
And believe with all my heart
For this is where the finding
Of hidden things must start.
And now just like the robin
My spirit soars and sings
Lifting up the truths that once
Were called the hidden things.

For several years I planned to call this book "The Hidden Things"
so the poem holds a special place in my heart.

A BUTTERFLY IN RUINS

A momentary life
amongst the broken stones
the butterfly in ruins
gleams in teeming tones.
From place to place it flutters
and everywhere it goes
the castle that is rubble
for an instant glows.
And I wonder if the butterfly
fears for anything
for now the ruined butterfly
has but a single wing.
No amount of money
can make it fly again.
Will e're another butterfly
venture where it's been?
The lonely wing is beating
throbbing as my heart
which like the ruined butterfly
is wholly torn apart.
Stupid butterfly
that among the ruins dies!
Stupid, stupid heart
that loud in anguish cries!

Grief is for me an overwhelming emotion . . .

SPIDER IN THE WIND

I wonder at the spider
hanging in the wind.
On one remaining strand
does its presence here depend.
Buffeted by forces
that it cannot control
the spider clings with purpose
for rebuilding is its goal.
To start anew when all is lost,
the spider's set on spinning
as also is the watcher
who seeks a new beginning.
The spider and the dreamer
never count the cost.
As long as you believe
a dream is never lost.
The world will tear apart,
mock and taunt, destroy,
while the dreamer builds again
and fills his heart with joy.
For – lo! – the wind has died
and the spider spins anew
which I who watch and dream
will also surely do.

and yet it is in man's nature to rebuild.

ON THE DOCK

With confidence I sit
And patiently I wait
For our relationship has been
A "go together" trait.
The ship cannot have left!
You would have had it stayed!
Yet there the churning wake
And I am sore dismayed.
But surely you'll return!
"Come back! Come back!" I cry
But as the day grows longer
I see your love's a lie.
The tears have cleared my vision
As dawn shines on the sea.
We both know there's no chance
That you'll return for me.
I am tired of fooling
With hoping and the waiting
And fearful for myself
For my heart is ripe for hating.
You have taken everything,
The love death couldn't shake.
I forgive and yet I now
Do it for my sake.
There is no ship with draw enough
To take to distant shore
The burden heavy in my heart
That I can bear no more.
And so among the flotsam
And jetsam I now leave
The bitterness and loneliness.
I can no longer grieve.
You have chosen life apart
And thus have made mine so.
I turn my back and eagerly
Into the world I go.
All that was before
Is memories of pain.
These I will not carry

Or look upon again.
For the sun upon the ocean
That you see today
Lights for me a brighter path
As I set out on my way.

Blessings you have taken all
And thus need none of mine.
Forgotten and forgotten
For both of us is fine.

The hardest step away,
The first has now been made
And with each follow subsequent
Which makes the sadness fade.

Freedom you have given me
To replace the love now lost
To be treasured always . . .

For I know too well the cost.

IF I WERE NOT A BEAR

"If I were not a bear,"
said the giant griz,
"I wouldn't swat you with my paw
and tell you how things is.
I wouldn't take the time
to teach you how to fish
or warn you that if something's free
there's poison in the dish.
If I were not a bear
I would still be game
'cause people hunt in banks.
They just change the name.
Don't believe them when they tell you,
'Naw! It ain't for money!'
I been a bear a lotta years
and there's always bees near honey.
They'd be trying to catch me
with interest rates and taxes.
You must be keen and vigilant
for when a bear or folk relaxes
the best that's gonna happen
is they'll end up in a zoo
and that's the very last thing
that I would wish for you.
Are you frightened, little cub?
My words were meant to scare
and remind you just how lucky
you are to be a bear!"

This poem reminds me of advice my father might have given me,
some of which I ignored and had to learn on my own.

AT PICKPOCKET DAM

I went traveling back in time
with my Mom today
about the times her cousins
and she went out to play.
It's been seven decades
since they rowed the lake.
Decisions and adventures
are the memories we make -
Swimming for the shore
to lie on sunny beaches
and faster for the fear
of those blood-sucking leaches!
They didn't get permission
but they acquired the key;
unlocked the boat the "Full-o-Fun"
and set out - bold and free!
I could hear their laughter
across the shallow pond
and join them in those happy days
we all must move beyond.
And listening and laughing
I was somehow there
for there are more happy times
in the memories we share.
So Mom, I want to thank you
for the trip out to the dam
and for your special love
that makes me who I am.

My mother told me this story in October 2016
over seventy years after it happened!

THE TWINKLE IN A WITCH'S EYE

"Beware the twinkle in a witch's eye!"
Said the one-eyed newt.
"Or if she stops to pinch you
And says, 'You're fat and cute!'
If she cackles, 'Stay for soup!'
You'd better turn and run
Unless to swim in boiling stew
Is your idea of fun!
Yes, she took an eye
But now I sure can see!
The twinkle in a witch's eye
Says she wants the rest of me!
It turns into a burning flame
Faster than a switch
So you'd better learn to recognize
And never trust a witch!"

LIAR AND THIEF

When you make a deal
With a liar and thief
Be certain and sure
It will lead you to grief.
For as they say leopards
Can't change their spots
And liars and thieves
Will always hatch plots.
Their lies will seem truer
Than truth itself does
And naught will return
To the way it once was.
Excuses will reign
And falsehood abound
For no one can tell
A lie by its sound.
Sweeter than sugar
And smoother than silk
Are the words you will hear

From the flattering ilk.
Woe for your wallet
And worse for your soul
Else like a dragon
They swallow you whole.

A NATURAL AT FLIGHT

I'm a natural at flight
But not like a bird
'Cause I usually just run
without saying a word.
Ofttimes I'm silent
When I do deign to stay
Which does as much good
As running away.
But there was one time
When I stood and I shouted
And as the words flew
I no longer doubted.
For courage is found
When a thought leaves your lips
And- FLASH! - in that instant
Cowardice flips!
Who am I kidding?
Who'll listen to me?
That matters not
As long as I'm free.
And as long as you're here -
Be not afraid! -
For with the sound of your voice
Courage is made.

For the title of this poem I picked two random words from a thesaurus!
Then I wrote the poem!

IVAN THE TERRIER
EATS A SNAKE

Ivan the Terrier
ate a snake
and I think it made
his tummy ache.
A piece was here!
Another there!
Ivan's stomach
didn't care.
Ivan looked -
oh! - so forlorn
but my sympathy
for him is torn.
For though the dinner
that he had
made him feel
so very bad
the dog just hasn't
got a clue
about what he should
and shouldn't do!
He was well
enough to play
so I let him out
just now, today.
He barked and ran
so happily
but in the distance
I did see

Ivan sniff!
And scratch!
And then --

Find and eat a snake again!

IVAN THE TERRIER
GETS LEFT BEHIND

We left him behind
in a kenneling place
where they said he could play
and have plenty of space.
"It's only four days,"
I said with a smile
but for such a small dog
that's quite a long while.
"He didn't eat much,"
they said when I came.
"He wouldn't chase balls
or play any game."
He looked a bit thinner
when they brought Ivan in
And I swear that dog talked!
"Don't ever do that again!
I'm not scared of much
as long as you're here.
Would you never come back?
That's my one only fear!"
I lifted up Ivan
as small as he was
and he licked my face!
That's just what he does.
"All is forgiven,"
his wagging stub said,
"and isn't it time
that I should be fed?"
And I laughed as I thought
and reached for a can,
"So loyal's the dog
and so lucky's the man!"

I began writing about Ivan the Terrier in 2003 after
a dream about our rat terrier, Neko.

A TREETOP CONVERSATION

I found myself in the top
of a tall, tall tree
where I had a conversation with
a wandering honeybee.
"Have I got some honey?
I thought you made the stuff!"
"Yeah. But demand is really high
and we can't produce enough.
I've spent my whole life working!
I'm tired of bee-ing busy.
Can I rest there in your palm?
I'm feeling kind of dizzy."
"Okay," I said and opened it.
"You won't sting me, will you?"
"If I do I'm dead!" it said.
"But it likely wouldn't kill you.
That's the way it seems to bee.
It's painful to fight back
so much so that most of us
would rather not attack.
But you're a giant human!
What have you got to fear?"
I put my finger to my lips
and held the bee quite near.
"Being human is not at all
a land of milk and honey
and most of us are like you bees
when faced with folks with money.
They promise to take care of us
but they take care of themselves
and some of us would trade to bee
a bee in some hive's shelves."
The bee looked at me in wonder.
It shook its head and grinned,
lifted up its little wings
and flew off in the wind.
And I think it must be happy,
free to fly away,
as I, too, seek a moment
to do the same today.

A HUNDRED YEARS AWAY

A poet lives a hundred years
or even more away
so never knows the rules
of the current day.
Imagination sweeps him
or her just like the tide
who learns that being different
can be a source of pride.
People wander by
oblivious to me
who longs for this thing only:
That they might better see.
Better see relationships
through the lens of love,
better see that charity
is what we need more of.
Better see that loyalty
to those both brave and true
though difficult and narrow
is the one way through.
And if my words have carried
for a hundred years
I hope today they'll bring you
laughter for your tears.
Life is but a shadow
of what will next ensue.
A hundred years from now
what will they think of you?
You alone can alter
this part of history's course.
Far off the river widens
but you are still its source.
So make today a special one
and do not bow to sorrow
and let the light inside of you
be your dawn tomorrow.

CATCHING THE HYSTERICAL MARE

I caught the hysterical mare
in town the other day
with nothing but an offering
of some plain old hay.
She ate it very quickly
as though she'd not been fed
but it did not seem to satisfy
the hefty quadruped.
She shook her head derisively
and flicked her silky mane,
looked at me and said,
"My boy, I hope I can explain.
I like telling jokes
and making people smile
more than giving rides.
That's just not my style!
People think it's crazy!
I'm not a normal horse
but giving happiness is good
no matter what the source.
So catch my show tomorrow
at noon out on the square!"
And not knowing what else to say
I said simply, "I'll be there."
The rain was pouring down
when I woke up from my dream
and thought the mare might like it
if I wrote upon her theme.
I scribbled everything
that I could recall
and went out to the barn
to see her in her stall.
But it was twelve o'clock
and she was gone, of course,
so I didn't get to hear the jokes
of the talking horse.
But she gave me opportunity
to imagine and to write
so I think I'll put some extra oats
in her feed tonight.

IVAN THE TERRIER
CHASES HIS TAIL

Ivan the Terrier
is chasing his tail.
It's just a short stub!
He must know that he'll fail!
But it's raining outside
and there's no place to run.
Chasing his tail
for Ivan is fun.
And as I watch I realize
it's also fun for me.
There are so many wonders
that Ivan helps me see.
I think back upon my life.
How does this apply?
When did I last do a thing
that did not need a "Why?"

Who says that fun must have
a purpose or a reason?

I propose that happiness
should always be in season!

For fun is pure and purposeful
of and on its own.
Save for Ivan's stub
I never would have known!
The puppy plays for fun alone
and treats life like a game
and thanks to little Ivan . . .

I can do the same.

THE PRICE FOR PEACE

It is in man's nature
to build and to destroy
and sadly it's the second
that too many more enjoy.

Power more than money
the sickest of sick seek
and it's to these the civilized
can't turn the other cheek.

There is a price for peace –
constant vigilance –
and however high the cost
well worth that expense.

For of justice, peace and mercy
none can stand alone.
Failure in but one of these
and with war we will atone.

Would the parties principal
who ceaselessly conspire
be more circumspect if they
were endangered by that fire?

Prosperity and peace
must be well protected
for with man's flaws 'tis certain
they'll never be perfected.

My sister Carol inspires me to write about peace.

THE PROGRESS
OF A THOUSAND YEARS

What makes men think it's noble
to die before their time?

War of any kind
is more than war; it's crime.

Machines and guns perfected
to maim, destroy and kill

yet armed with only sticks and stones
the same as Cain, man will.

There is just no logic
once the fighting starts

giving rise to hatred
in what were kindly hearts.

Where will someone live
when their home's destroyed?

When love's displaced from human hearts
anger fills the void.

And then the cycle starts again.
The weak become the strong.

The history of man has been
exchanging wrong for wrong.

Nothing can be built
lest there be peace before.

The progress of a thousand years
is lost in just one war.

THE JOY OF GREATEST WONDER

It used to be the two of us
who traveled far and wide
to talk of things and laugh
or simply sit beside.
But now the times have called us
each separately away
though you are always in my thoughts
throughout each passing day.
Still together in our aims
and deep within our hearts
but without you by my side
I sleep in stops and starts.
Oh, my love! What force the world
has brought itself to bear
on we two whose only thought
was, "Everything to share!"
We will persevere
for our promises we'll keep
for the earth has never seen a love
like ours so true and deep.
What trial and tribulation
try to tear asunder
is stronger now than ever,
a joy of greatest wonder!
The two of us have pledged
to share the self-same cup
and in the fiercest storms
to hold each other up.
For hardship we are closer
than we ever were before,
two spirits bound in love
both now and evermore.

STRUGGLES WITH THE WIND

A ship tacks quickly
Left and right
As it and winds
That move it fight.
Quickly, nimbly
Sometimes and
Others clumsily by hand,
But for skill
Of captain, crew,
Capsize it would
Likely do.
Some would fear
As it lists
But – there! –it exits
From the mists.
First one way
And then the other
As struggle we
With wind another.
Many times
We've done this now
So trouble not
For we know how.
Tire not of
Salt and spray
And forward look
For there's the bay
Girded from
The wind by shore
There to rest
And to explore.
Each is free
A home to build
As freedom's promise
Is fulfilled.

THE POET'S MISFORTUNES

Poets get the hard stuff.
That's pretty much expected.
Most of life they spend
ignored and rejected.
Not enough money
to keep bankers at bay
so poets have visions
of running away.
Some of them do
like Byron and Keats
but to run is not remedy
for internal defeats.
The poetic soul
is a dangerous place
for adversity follows
keeping the pace.
Bankruptcy! Scandal!
Reputation destroyed!
From tribulation
a poet's employed.
Not always wiser
with nickels and dimes,
the poet is watcher
and recorder of times.
He ventures forth
beyond his own hand
trying to catch
the mood of the land.
And this to achieve
he journeys alone
thus putting at risk
the loves of his own.
Tragedy travels
wherever he goes
and he cannot escape it
with disguises or clothes.
And perhaps the one difference
between others and he
is that for his misfortunes
the poet can see.

SIXTY-SEVEN POETS

Sixty-seven poets
Seeking one position
Each of us quite sure
Of his style and mission.
Sending in our poems
As if it really mattered
Hoping it's our moniker
Across the headlines splattered.
Our fans and friends spur us on
And we write and write some more
Yet must remember that it's truth
A poem's written for.
And then it doesn't matter
Who wins the golden prize
Unless it's in the light
From your reader's eyes.
Sixty-seven poets
Trying to be great
Have somehow manufactured
Number sixty-eight.

Occasionally I am told that a student in a class I've addressed has decided
to become a writer. I am sure other writers have had the same experience.
I wrote this poem when I applied to be *poet laureate* for the state of Missouri.
I didn't get it but at least I have that position in the City of Byrnes Mill!

THE PIG AND THE PROPHET

The pig never liked it
when the prophet came near
for the words that were spoken
it cared not to hear.
"You're gonna be breakfast
on the farmer's good plate.
Make a run for the woods
before it's too late!"
It tried to ignore
the prophet's advice
but when the gate was left open
it didn't think twice!
And now there are signs
that show the pig's face.
"It is destructive
so we all must give chase!"
And I think of the chances
I've had to be free
and how they have tried
to "pigify" me.
So I bowed my neck
for thirty-three years
'til the gate was ajar!
Then I conquered my fears.
And what's left of me
won't ever go back
so as for the pig
don't ask me to track.
I ain't gonna do it
though that pig may be bad
'cause it finally escaped
and that makes me glad!

There are signs along the highways that ask for help
catching the feral pigs that roam the countryside.
I wouldn't know what to do if I saw one, except maybe run!

MY HOMEWORK

A monkey didn't eat it
or in a fit of rage
rip it into pieces
bit by bit and page by page.
There were no monkey ninjas
with swords of samurai.
My teacher always knows it
when I tell a boldfaced lie.
So I turned my homework in
but I wish instead I hid it
'cause from the grade I got
she thinks the monkey did it!

THERE ARE SKUNKS
AND THERE ARE SKUNKS

Do skunks spray other skunks?
Rarely so I hear
And only when they're desperate
With anger or in fear.
When I found this out
It made me pause and think
For people who are smarter
Can make a bigger stink.
A skunk restrains itself
For what other skunks can do
And we would lead more peaceful lives
If people did that, too.

INTO THE LION'S EYES

I have looked into the lion's eyes.
Ferociously they shine!
Like the wounded antelope
I hear them say, "You're mine!"
There is a place beyond, below
the conscious mind so deep
one that only lion's eyes
can waken from its sleep.

"Live!" it cries.
"Survive!"
"Rise up from your pain!"

My heart beats wildly now
yet frozen, I remain.
I hear the lion roar
as it saunters towards the kill
and there is but one option:

To conquer fear with will!

And though my side is bleeding
I quickly leap away
before the lion's eyes
can claim me as their prey.
I am stronger now
and wiser for my foe
and for the hidden parts of me
that I have come to know.
I escaped the lion's eyes
and I no longer doubt
the strength of spirit deep within
nor the greater One without.

IVAN THE TERRIER AND
THE GERMAN SHEPHERD

I put Ivan on a leash
when we go for a walk
or else he might leap as high
as an eagle or a hawk.
He gets so excited
exploring with his nose
that he forgets to watch
the places that he goes.
There was a German Shepherd
on the path the other day
that wagged its tail expecting
Ivan to come and play.
But Ivan's nose was in the grass.
He was preoccupied
but with the shifting wind
his eyes snapped open wide.
He jumped and yapped and barked
trying to attack
but it didn't take much effort
to hold little Ivan back.
The German Shepherd looked at me
then at the little dog
and with its tail and head held high
continued on its jog.
Ivan looked at me quite proudly,
sure he'd saved the day,
and since I still remember it
he must have, in a way.

Ivan looked into the German Shepherd's eyes and was not afraid.
What an inspiration!

PICKLE PIE

The other day I had a piece
of Granny's pickle pie.
No one else would eat it
so I asked my Granny, "Why?"
She answered with a question.
"Did it taste good to you?"
I said that it did
and she took my word as true.
"Well," she said, "the name is what
most folks can't abide.
It's like judging folks by looks
instead of what's inside.
The ingredients are secret
and, indeed, you'll never know
how a person's been affected
by what happened long ago.
Listen and observe.
Be open to advice.
Do you like my pickle pie?
Then have another slice!"

WHY WHITE CRAYONS?

To draw and color pictures
on paper that is black
or when you make mistakes
to try to take them back.
For writing a message
if you are a spy!
I discover reasons
every time I try.
But you had to ask
for me to do that
else the question would be
right back where it sat.
Sometimes it takes

a voice loud and clear
to make people question
the words that they hear
or the choices they're offered
and think their own way
and that's why your asking
helped me today.
To color a snowflake
individually
so it's not just the blizzard
but discrete things I see.
Why do I ponder
and write about this?
Because if I didn't
there'd be so much I'd miss!

LEARNING JAPANESE

I spent a little time
learning Japanese.
"Arigato" means "Thank you."
"Dozo" is for "Please."
I learned to count to ten
with a relative of ease
but I forgot what to say
when someone makes a sneeze.
Learning language often comes
slowly, in degrees,
and I'm glad I do not know
how to torment or to tease.
But I do know how to smile
and everyone agrees
that's one language sure to reach
across the widest seas.

THE RISE OF THE AFTERNOON GOAT

The early bird gets the worm
before the sun gets hot
and so the goats fight for food
but I see one does not.
It sits in the shade of the willow tree
beside the babbling brook
as calm and still as a statue
so I prolong my look.
I watch it all through the morning
as it nibbles on bits of hay
with an eye on the morning goats
as they battle for half of the day.
And then, its rivals exhausted
and their tummies touching the ground,
the afternoon goat arises
with a jump, a leap and a bound!
It's time for the evening feeding
and the afternoon goat's at the trough
with a fierce and obstinate nature
that drives all the morning goats off.
And I must admit I'm surprised
that a goat could have such a plan,
to change its behavior on purpose
which is more than many men can.
A strategy filled with deception!
Intentions deftly concealed!
And the rise of the afternoon goat
has made it the king of the field!

I made these observations while guests were feeding
the baby goats at Grant's Farm.

MY NEW HARMONICA

I bought a new harmonica
At the store the other day.
When I get home from school
I can't wait to play.
I practiced in the afternoon
And well into the night.
If I rehearse like that each day
I just might get it right!
I think my momma's proud of me!
She had tears welling in her eyes.
Perhaps my dedication
Caught her by surprise.
I left it on the table
And it's waiting there for me
But someone must have stolen it!
It's gone!
Where could it be?
My mother says it's tragic
And she wishes that she knew
So I'd better tell the garbage man.
I heard him playing, too!

BANANAS IN AUGUST

Bananas in August
aren't my favorite treat
especially when they're left
too long in the heat.
I tell you that to warn you
as you take your seat
I haven't been out shopping
and that's all there is to eat.

NIBBLING ON PAPER

I nibbled on paper
As I am prone to do
And ate half the phone book
Before my meal was through.
I swallowed a thesaurus,
A dictionary, more
Paper than I'd eaten
At any time before.
I ate two reams at the office,
One blue and one red!
They were all out of orange
So I ate two purple instead.
And now my boss is telling me
My habit is wasteful and silly
So I look at the copies he told me to make
And answer him wryly,

"OH, REALLY?"

AND SOMETIMES Y

A, E, I, O and U
are consistently vowels.
"But what about me?"
Y sometimes howls.
"I'm a good vowel
with consonant skills!"
I looks to U and says,
"It's forgotten its pills."
Yes, try to be different
in some little way
and you can be sure
that's what folks will say.
It can be whether
you wear sandals or shoes
or what station you watch

to gather the news.
It can be hair.
What color? How long?
Sometimes it's different!
Not right and not wrong.
Nevertheless,
people need something to blame.
So, hey! I can't help it!
I've got a "Y" in my name.

A SANCTUARY MOOD

Lately I have been
in a sanctuary mood
as civilization is
apparently unglued.
There is no place to go
where fright won't follow me
and I fear the tide
of rising anarchy.
And so I must now face
the things I would avoid
discarding those I value
and have most enjoyed.
And in my desperation
I pause to say a prayer
and surprisingly I find
a sanctuary there.
There's solace in the silence
for here I am surrounded
by the Spirit's love which says
my fears are all unfounded.

The love within me's greater
than the evil that's without
and sanctuary is a faith
that never has a doubt.

THE APOSTROPHE SONG

It's a long name
for a very small thing,
a dot in the air
dragging a string.
There isn't a sound
like a letter conveys
but it is important
in two different ways.
One is possessive.
It says, "This is mine!"
The other states plainly,
"These two words combine."
Belonging together
is what life's all about
and the apostrophe says,
"Let's remove any doubt!
I'm yours and you're mine!
We together belong
in true love forever!"
That's the apostrophe song.

NIGGLING NUISANCES

Inconsequential nuisances
Can also be called "niggling"
Like the coins there in your pocket
That you are always jiggling.
The way you twitch your nose
When you're nervous like a cat
And how you tap your foot –
Who puts up with that?
I wish there were a way
You could see you like I do.
You just might appreciate
What I am going through.
But I take the higher road.

I try to keep the peace
Hoping that these nuisances
Decline and finally cease.
Yes, you're the lucky one!
On you the blessings pour
Since I don't have those habits:

WHAT DO YOU MEAN, I SNORE?

QUACK LIKE A DUCK

Last night while I was talking
An odd idea struck:
It doesn't make much sense
To say, "Quack like a duck!"
Since the only other being
To ever make that sound
Is a human one,
Not horse nor cat nor hound.
Why does one waste four words
When one does well enough?
Aren't there more important things
Than such silly stuff?
Use your words judiciously!
Do not waste them so,
Something I should have thought of
A couple of minutes ago. . .

And if I had then
I would not have written this poem!

VICTORY'S MOMENTS

Most often the reward
for a race well-run
is another stance
before a starting gun.
The competition's tougher
but I know that going in
and realize life gets harder
especially if I win.
For though a golden medal
around my neck be placed
it only takes one loss
for my fame to be erased.
But today I was the first
to cross the finish line
and no matter what else happens
that instant will be mine.
There's never rest for weary ones
and glory quickly fades
so treasure victory's moments
and not her accolades.
For it is in the striving
that victory is found
and in the pride that follows
she is so often bound.

BANANAS IN SEPTEMBER

I made banana bread
with bananas in September,
the ones I bought in August.
I hope you don't remember!

VICTORY VICTORY BEGETS

Today is the end of all things as they were
and the beginning of all things new.
Today it matters not what you did
but rather what you'll do.
Right now is the time to say goodbye
to the life that you have known,
to disregard your cautiousness
and finally strike out on your own.
It is the time for courage
that you've sought so many years
enough so that this once
you can conquer all your fears.
Winning just once is a start
for victory victory begets.
Better to win this one day
then to live a life of regrets.
I write this advice as to you
but it is to myself I address
for I must both act and believe
most of all to achieve true success.
Today is the day I lose all
on which I ever depended
and I wonder why I held on
so long to a life that had ended.

BANANAS IN OCTOBER

Bananas in October
bought in August sure do stink
and I wish I hadn't hidden them
underneath the sink!

WILL AND CAN AND DO

In the local library
I talked a bit too loud
and was told that's not how one should want
to stand out from the crowd.
And thus I spent these many years
working silently
waiting for someone to grant
such opportunity.
Fifty years or more it's been
and here I sit so still
until at last I realize
I'm the only one who will.
It's hard to break the habits
that I have learned so well

but I will and can and do

for there is much I have to tell:

Stories I have kept inside
and held in check too long
breaking free and making me
like them, brave and strong.

It is now my turn
and though I won't be rude
from this day on I promise
a brand-new attitude.
And if I speak too loudly
it will be for what is good
and it just might be a better world
if everybody would.

FUKUSHIMA

The wave is always bigger
than the castle made of sand
and overwhelms the walls
however well they're planned.

This I saw with children's eyes
at the edges of the sea
and found that there were powers
stronger much than me.

So how is it, I wonder,
that men so learned and bright
try to tame the ocean
yet know they'll lose that fight.

Katrina. Fukushima.
Where will it be next?
And why will the new disaster
leave us all perplexed?

We pretend that it is only
preparedness and will
until nature wins again
with a wave that's bigger still.

But we will build it back,
the ask not if but when,
with pride that rises like a wave
just to fall again.

WHEN PHYLLIS DYED HER HAIR

She was naturally blond
But wanted it brunette
So in the barn she painted it
Then let it dry and set.
She went back to the kitchen
Smiling and so proud
Until her mother saw her
And gave a shriek so loud
It caused the cattle to stampede
In pastures two miles down
And people thought that sirens
Were going off in town.
Her hair was short that summer
And well into the fall
And her mother was quite lucky
To have any left at all.
What she had was white
After all that she'd been through
And when Phyllis dyed her hair
Her mother dyed hers, too.

GROWING IN THE SHADE

I was happy in the shade.
It was all I knew
and protected from the wind and rain
tall and strong I grew.
For always there beside me
was a taller tree
that grew its roots for many years
and cleared a place for me.
But then it lost its branches
in a storm last night
and I feel the power

of growing in the light.
"It is now your time,"
the old tree seems to say
and so I spread my branches
fully on display.
I am now the one
to catch the rising wind
offering protection
to the saplings as they bend.
The old tree watches proudly
as its job is finally done
as I who grew in shade
now prosper in the sun.

OUT OF THE BOX

Today I have decided
to live outside the box
and because of that I must be
clever like a fox.
Why can't I be different
without the consequence?
For sometimes brand new methods
make a lot of sense!
It's a struggle every day
to lift that heavy lid
but I can make a difference
and be proud of what I did.
And though they hunt me like a fox
and keep me on the run
I am free to think and dream
and that means I have won.

I wrote this while at the Conference of the Young Years at
the Lake of the Ozarks in central Missouri. A presenter
used it in her talk just a few minutes later.

AN ODE TO A STORE

Like everything on earth
its days are numbered few
for a lifetime lifts as quickly
as the morning dew.
Yet as I sit so quietly
and people march on past
I sense this store's impression
is one that's made to last.
More than bricks and mortar
there is a spirit here
that people will remember.
It fills their hearts with cheer.
And anything that does
such an awesome thing
will live again like blossoms
blooming in the spring.
For sometime in the future
an idea someone caught
will manifest itself
becoming more than thought.
"Just a little store."
"Such a silly name!"
Yet calls out through the ages,
"My life will not be tame!
For even though I'm only
a tiny little store
the passions I instill
will live forevermore!"

I made many friends during the six years Sharon and I ran
the **I Don't Want to Kiss a Llama!** store. Sometimes people would
visit and bring ideas in. Kathi Goersh was one of those and she
inspired many poems including "The Dinosaur's Lingerie", and "The
Chubby Dinosaur" and "Cheesecake, Chess and Carousel Ponies"
series of poems. Thanks to all who supported us there!

WORDS LIKE WINGS

Its wingtip nearly touched me
as it floated on the air
and soundlessly it passed
leaving me aware
of what my senses miss
and how close by might be
fate that reaches out
to raise or ruin me.
And so I wander on my way
up the long steep grade
once again unsure
how decisions long since made
perhaps determine who I am
and what I think and do
yet leave me as before
without a single clue
save the silent flight itself
that, oh, so quickly flashed,
for words like wings can take us
on journeys unabashed
by the boom and bellow
of the common grind
instead to fly quite silently
and touch the higher mind.
It contradicts my poetry
for it's muted not verbose
yet the eagle's silent flight
brings me, oh, so close
to understanding
then quickly flies away
leaving me to wonder
and wander through my day.

THE CONNECTION

There's a connection
between left brain and right
that opens a portal
in the dead of the night.
Logical thoughts
and imagination collide
touching each other
like the sand and the tide.
And raised from the deep
a mystery lies.
Walk on the beach
and open your eyes!
For what the tide carries
it carries away
and buries again
in the depths of the bay.
And only the pilgrim
who searches at dawn
will know of these things
before they are gone.
So attend to the stories
that the travelers tell
for their time and your time
are fleeting as well.

When I wake up with the memory of a dream
I give it a title and write about it at the first opportunity.

SHRINK NOT FROM THE HEIGHTS

The eagle shrinks not from the heights
nor do depths a fish dismay
and when obstacles arise for me
I will not turn away.
For as the eagle and the fish
suit well for sky and sea
so I find persistence
is a natural part of me.
For though sometimes defeated
I know not surrender
and so find victory ultimate
in its finest splendor.
And where I've fallen short
I cast a marker down –
Here I ventured unafraid
that I would crash or drown.
And from this place and time I see
that for my force of heart
where my mission ended
is, for someone else, a start
and a place to launch
a campaign of their own
for as a man does dare to dream
he does not dream alone.

I first published my own poems in 2003.
Others have told me that this is an inspiration for them.

WORDS ON THE LOOSE

My old thesaurus split in half
with ten years hence of use
and all the words spilled out
so now they're running loose.
I catch them as I can
when they wander by
but I can't grasp them all
no matter how I try.
I remember our dog Lucky
and how he ran away
and instead of chasing him
I knelt as if to pray.
I called his name and held my arms
– oh! – so wide apart.
I depended not upon my legs
but rather on his heart.
And so he wagged his tail
and licked my happy face.
I love it when the words
come seeking my embrace.
That's how I got the words
to the book back in
but I kind of hope it breaks
and they get away again.

THINGS I BETTER NOT DO

Chase a distant star.
Think outside the box.
Shake a static world
Creating aftershocks.
Give up all I have
To try to catch a dream
Or struggle with the current
Of a rising stream.
Try again when failure
Has put me down for good

And stand up one more time
When no one thought I could.
Try to live forever
With words that rhyme and sing
And show through dark of winter
The advent of the spring.
Dare defend the standard
Of truth and honesty
And strive against the perils
That so beset the free.
Make a declaration
That I will stand apart
And share the inspiration
From deep within my heart.
These are things convention says
That I must never do
Yet I'll try every one of them
Before my life is through.

NUM NUM THE TURTLE

Num Num the turtle
constantly craved
to go to the parlor
and have his nails shaved.
But he wanted a rub
on his backside as well
which could not be done
because of his shell.
So lonely and sad
he shaved his own nails
and sometimes the sense
in poetry fails.

Two girls visited the **I Don't Want to Kiss a Llama!** store
and gave me this idea and the one for "Harry the Hamster".

ON THE LAST DAY OF SCHOOL

I'll tell my teacher what I think,
That English, math and spelling stink,
That though I smiled all year through
I like school like doggy-poo!
I'll toss my food when we're at lunch
And on the playground throw a punch!
I'll take each and every dare!
What teachers think I do not care!
That's what I will do today
And I'll get started right away.
But -Oops!-my teacher saw this note
And she says before I gloat
She's going to take a closer look
At me in her grading book.
She says to follow every rule
Unless I'm liking summer school!
And since I'd really like to pass

I'll be good today in class!

OSCAR AND MOLASSES

Oscar was my goat
on the farm back then
and when I smell molasses
my thoughts go back again.
Oscar knew that I had
molasses cubes in hand
and when he heard my truck
he'd run across the land.
Past the cows and pasture
and underneath the fence,
the goat was better than a dog
detecting those sweet scents.
He never ran like that
for anyone but me
because he knew I'd give away

the treats I brought for free.
And though it may have been
just a goat's sweet tooth
he made me feel real special
and that's the honest truth.

A guest at Grant's Farm told me about the goat he had as a boy.

UNTIL IT'S GONE

"I feel so old," he said
when he was seventeen
which to me at seventy
seems a bit obscene.
I watched him run a mile
in just five minutes flat
and remembered when it seemed
that I was fast like that.
"I would have run it faster
but I have a muscle strain."
I guess it didn't take him long
to learn how to complain.
He's getting pretty good
at discerning what is wrong
and fixing which is fine
when you are young and strong.
As for me the years that passed
I hope have made me wise
enough to know this worldly realm
gives no compromise.
So here's a bit of wisdom
from one who's gone before,
until it's gone you didn't know
what your youth was for.

STATUES BY A ZOMBIE

Michelangelo he was
to the zombie hoard
and they're hoping his great icon
may one day be restored.
He built it using earwax
from a sickly pachyderm
and the image of his finger
plucking makes me squirm.
He made a model twelve feet tall
of the president
but it melted on a sunny day
and down the drain it went.
Elephants are endangered now
and their earwax is forbidden
so the zombies seek another trove
similarly hidden.
They scatter out in groups
of seventy or more
and I've learned that they are closing in
on what they're looking for.
And if the clump there on your finger
is any kind of clue
you'd better clean your ears

BEFORE THE ZOMBIES DO!

BANANAS IN NOVEMBER

Bananas bought in August
discovered in November
are the main ingredients
for my fruitcake in December!

WHEN THE QUEEN SHOOK HER FINGER

When the queen shook her finger
To the crowd that assembled
It wasn't just they
But the whole nation who trembled.
They saddled the horses
Of ten thousand knights,
Closed all the schools
And turned out the sprites
Who spilled into the streets
Chanting and waving,
"Give the queen what she wants!
It must be worth saving!"
All she proposed
Did the Parliament pass
And in every pub
They lifted a glass
In grand celebration
And joy, I suppose,
For reasons each man
On the living earth knows.
When the queen shakes her finger
A thousand ships sail!
The king himself trembles,
Sits down and goes pale.
For in every palace
And common homes, too,
The queen rules the roost!
It's sad, but quite true.

CHILDREN'S DAY

Of course we have a Mother's Day
and everyone knows why,
and there also is a Father's Day
for how hard they always try.
But we wanted a day just for us,
one we could call our own.
We thought that we should have it now
and not wait 'til we were grown.
"Daddy, there's no Children's Day!
Please won't you tell us why?"
"Every day is Children's Day!"
was my father's frank reply.
We didn't like the answer,
no presents under a tree,
but my father lived out what he said
in ways we all could see.

It was Children's Day on holidays
spent together at the beach
and when we needed help at school
Daddy always stopped to teach.
He held us on his shoulders.
He lifted us one and all
and we could touch the sky from there!
My God, he was so tall!
We hiked together on mountain trails
as we children changed and grew.
He led us on the path of life,
let us go and off we flew.
But he loved it when we lit again
like returning doves
for a father never loses
his love for those he loves.

Can Children's Day survive
as old times fade away?
The answer's in their laughter
as the children run and play.
Their Grandpa knew that play and fun
were cures for many ills

and that will help their parents too,
so put down your work and bills!
Spend time now with your children
to teach what's wrong and right,
and tell them that you love them
as you tuck them in tonight.
For our children are a treasure
who in our hearts will stay
when we cheer and celebrate
every day as Children's Day.

Yes, my father actually said and believed those words . . .

OLD MAN SLEEPING

Old man sleeping. Dangerous.
His mind's filled up with dreams.
Too weak to hold them back
they spill out through its seams.
He whispers them to children
in a story or a tale
whose hands and hearts renew
what long were weak and frail.
The man keeps telling stories.
He knows 'tis not too late
for a parable is precious
and its power truly great.
Old man speaking. Passionate.
Puts everyone to sleep
and as they dream the children
decide which ones to keep.

This poem is based on a comment texted to my brother Clyde
and perhaps on my tiring more quickly these days . . .

OIL AND WATER

"That new kitten's ears
Seem so very long
And its meow sounds like a growl!
I hope that nothing's wrong.
It likes to chase a ball
And sometimes to chase me
But that nose is just too huge!
I wonder, can it see?
Perhaps its feeling lonely
For it really is quite strange.
Maybe if I play with it
Its mood would start to change."

"That's the oddest puppy
That I have ever known.
I've seen dogs with spots before
But not the stripes it's grown!
I've never heard it bark,
Just a whimper now and then,
And it really does smell different.
I wonder where it's been!
I suppose if I can just look past
Its idiosyncrasies,
It could be my friend
As long as there's no fleas!"

The kitten and the puppy dog
Have formed an odd alliance
For oil and water do not mix.
I learned that in science!
What one sees in the other
Is what happens in return,
A lesson from two baby pets
That people ought to learn.
I watch them romp and run,
See how happily they play,
And wish there were more people
Who saw the world that way.

Written as our cat Star and puppy Neko played together.

THE KETTLE, THE POT AND WHAT THEY WERE NOT

The pot thought the kettle was a bit too black.
The kettle looked at the pot and saw a crack.
Isn't it funny they both had a knack
to see faults in the other without looking back?

The horse hates how the donkeys gather and bray.
The donkeys all sneer when they hear a neigh.
Neither will listen whatever they say
and they both think that living like that is okay.

The cat thought the dog barked too loud.
The dog hated the cat for how it meowed.
Friendship between them they never allowed.
To forgive or forget they were much too proud.

You look at me in utter dismay
and I wonder at your sorry display.
Each of us wishes the other away
and we must each change that. Now! Today!

The black helped the kettle cook really hot.
In spite of the crack the pot held a lot.
Once each saw this they anger forgot
for both what they were and what they were not.

I originally published this poem in 2004
in my collection called ***Climb the Red Mountain***.

SAIL WITH ME TOMORROW

Sail with me tomorrow
and feel the mist and spray
for the wind is strong behind us
and the sun sparkles on the bay.
From the river's mouth we'll sail
and set our course far out to sea.
The ebbing tide is pulling us
so won't you sail with me?
The clouds on the horizon
mean naught to hardy souls
for our ship will never founder
or break upon the shoals.
The is no path to follow!
Our destination's not yet known
and just the two of us will go!
At last we're on our own.
But that's the price of freedom.
We must leave the place we know
yet when we hear the ocean's call
we will surely go.
So sail with me tomorrow
on a trip to forever's shores
as you look into my eyes
and I get lost in yours.

I LOVE YOU IN THE SUMMER RAIN

The sun shines down through cotton clouds.
There's a special glow about this place
but ne'er compares to my heart's delight,
the sunshine of your face.
The birds are chirping merrily
as they dart from tree to tree
but it's the sound of your sweet laughter
that brings heaven's joys to me.
I feel the warmth of raindrops
and smell the sweetness of the land

yet such will never fill my heart
as when you touch my hand.
I love you in the summer rain
that sparkles in the mist
and settles gently on the rose
as with a diamond it were kissed.
Oh, that we could share this day again
in heavenly refrain
for I will love you always
just as now, here, in the summer rain.

JUST ONE STAR

Just one star in all the heavens
like a diamond in the night,
one star's my only vision,
one star my only light.
Just one flower in the garden,
such beauty it bestows,
a barren field made bountiful
graced by a single rose.
I hold it to my ear,
the single shell upon the shore,
the single voice that calls,
"Come with me I'll show you more."
I follow where it leads me
to see if it is true.
It is! For here in all the world
my only one is you.
Just one star in all the heavens,
one shell in all the sea,
you're the flower that's most beautiful
and the only one for me.

These poems were also published in **Climb the Red Mountain**.

ALL OF HEAVEN

How came I to love you so
when you were just a thought?

Before your hands could hold me
I by your heart was caught.

What knew I of beauty
e'er I saw your form?

I loved you in a dream, my love,
and that has kept me warm.

All the joy and happiness
that I thought I knew

I now lay aside
to devote myself to you.

And what of time the spoiler
who our days devours?

All falls to his swinging sword
save this love of ours.

So stretch your hand and touch me.
Feel my heart began to race!

For I see all of heaven
when I behold your face.

Regarding love poems, I wrote a Mother's Day poem in grade school
and my Mom still has it! I wrote "Barefoot on Roses" for Sharon in 2003 and used it
as a guide for *I Don't Want to Kiss a Llama!* It is in the latest edition of that book.

AN OLD MAN'S CAVEAT

"What's the answer?" I was asked
by a younger man.
"What am I to do when things
alter from the plan?"
"Love," I said reactively
e'er I could even think.
"To mend the bonds of brotherhood
love's the vital link."
Then we both fell silent
in embarrassment perhaps
at an old man's folly
and seeming mental lapse.
And I have lately pondered
upon what I had said
and decided that in every life
love's the daily bread.
"Folly upon folly!"
I hear the cynics say.
"What about the enemies
who attack us every day?"
I know too well the answer,
to fight the fire with fire,
yet even when we must our aim
should make our hearts look higher.
Love can break the cycle
like no weapon can
and is the sole alternative
to the wars of man.
So meditate upon
this old man's caveat,
that the answer's always love
even when it's not.

THE SEMICOLON

It's not like a period
that's used to end a sentence
nor does it say what came before
is a reason for repentance.
But there are times in life
it pays to hesitate;
the semicolon symbol says,
"Why not deliberate?"
It allows new thought
with an altered direction;
sometimes it's a way
to make a correction.
"I choose to be different
so I'm taking a pause
to fix and accept
some of my flaws.
And in so doing I will find
the parts of me most true
which is what, in our lives,
each of us must do."

THE BIGGEST ZOO

They have the strongest gorillas
And ten of the tallest giraffes.
Their elephants are bigger than whales
And outweigh all others by halfs.
When the lions roar at their loudest
You have to cover your ears
And the baboons are really the grossest
'Cause they have the reddest of rears.
And on a holiday evening
It's crowded as crowded can be.
I'm trying to park in the car
And everyone's yelling at me!
Their jabber reminds me of monkeys
Hanging from top of the cage
And I've never seen lion or tiger

Lose control in that kind of a rage.
I haven't walked through the gate
But I feel as I've already been
'Cause thanks to the people's behavior
It's a bigger zoo outside than in!

THE KING AND THE ROOSTER

The king was so used
to getting his way
and commanded the rooster
crow late in the day.
He was mad in the morning
when it yodeled at dawn.
"Off with its head!"
he said with the a yawn.
They gathered the hatchets
and set out in search
but too late for the rooster
had abandoned its perch.
It flew far away
yet it still dared to crow
so long and so loud
to let the king know
that in spite of his throne,
his scepter and crown
to the rooster he's not
the toast of the town.
Life humbles us all
be we pauper or king
which is why that old rooster
continues to sing.

THE CAT
AND THE GIANT SUNBEAM

She can spend all morning
in the selfsame place
for in the giant sunbeam
there are no rats to chase.
The shadows are so slow
to creep across the floor
as through the giant sunbeam
the warmth and light both pour.
She purrs, she mews, she flicks her tail
and opens up her eyes.
It seems that her position
in the sun has made her wise.
"Do what makes you happy
while you can," submits the cat
and I resolve that for today
I will do just that!

THE EXTRA EYE

The tuatara's extra eye
is just a little dot
but I suppose it's good
for tiny things to spot.
It makes us people envy them
but I say we should not
until we learn to use
both the eyes we've got.

I learned about the tuatara from one of Ryan's grade school projects.

ON DOING NOTHING

I don't have anything to do
with the wind that moves the leaves
or with the rain that falls
and the thirsty ground receives.
I don't have to pet the dog.
She's glad to sit with me
as if to say it's fine
not to do, but be.
The sun is shining brightly.
The temperature's just right.
If I'm still perhaps a dream
will visit me tonight.
"What will be will be,"
my mind and body say
as peace past understanding
settles down today.
I am doing nothing.
The pen writes on its own
to tell me in my reverie
that I am not alone.
The wind and rain are guided
by a greater hand
and doing nothing helps me
to also understand
that like the leaves I am moved
by forces greater than
all and any concepts
from the mind of man.
Succumb to them I will
and welcome them I do
as I lie here doing nothing
and the spirit passes through.

THE CAT AND THE EGG ON THE TABLE

I left an egg on the table
To see what just might occur
If perhaps our striped gray tabby
Would hatch it under her fur.
I thought it would be an experience
That we would never forget
So I showed the egg to the cat
And gave it a spin where it set.
I left and went on to work
With nary a thought in my head
About the fate of the egg
And what might happen instead.
That evening as I arrived home
I discovered an odious stinking
And as I clean up the mess I wonder,
"What in the world was I thinking?"

THE OWLS IN THE CHIMNEY

The owls in the chimney
Built their nest one fall.
They didn't seem to notice
The fireplace at all.
They didn't even bother
To ask or to inquire
What things might occur
Should we start a fire.
They weren't the best of neighbors,
Hooting through the night,
But at least when we had company
They stayed out of sight.
And compared to all the human
Neighbors we have had
I have to say the owls
Weren't all that bad.

THE CATERPILLAR'S CUBICLE

The caterpillar's cubicle
Was right next to mine
And its evaluations
Said its work was fine.
But one day it decided
To slither down the hall,
The day that they were vacuuming
Which was not good at all.
They cleaned out its cubicle
Yesterday at noon
And say they'll do the same to mine
If sales don't pick up soon.
But no one has the money
'Cause work is hard to find.
If I lose my job
I just might lose my mind.
"It's all about the bottom line,"
They tell me with a wink
But I know for sure they don't care
If I swim or sink.
And I hope the caterpillar
Grew wings and flew away
'Cause that is what I would like
To do myself today.

BANANAS IN JANUARY

Bananas I bought in August
which she found in January
are why my fiancé now says
she's not sure she wants to marry!

SAID FROM THE SHADE

As I stood there sweltering
In the sultry summer sun
A voice said from the shade,
"We'll have great loads of fun!"
Mine replied in anguish,
"It's getting pretty hot,"
But the voice from in the shade
Assured me it was not.
I sat there doing nothing
And the voice said in surprise,
"Get off of your behind
And get some exercise!"
"I think . . . I need some water . ."
"No, you've got it made,"
Came the sympathetic
Voice out of the shade.
"Really," I complained,
"I think I'm going to faint."
"Now you're being silly," said the voice,
"'Cause you know you ain't!"
"You should be feeling better,"
The shady voice foretold,
"'Cause there's a breeze today
And I'm getting kind of cold."
That was the final straw.
I couldn't stand it anymore
So I quickly ran inside
And slammed and locked the door.
"You'll be sorry," said the voice.
"It's a lovely afternoon."
But with the rising temperatures
It quickly changed its tune.
It's possible I heard that voice.
"Let me in!" it cried,
One of those annoying sounds
That air conditioners hide.

A RAGGED RAINCOAT

As I prepare to hazard
A course in dreary gloom
Perchance I spy a raincoat
In the corner of the room.
On close examination
I find it rather worn
And behold a section of one sleeve
That is badly torn.
But the drops against the window
And the howling of the wind
Make a ragged raincoat
My unexpected friend.
I gather it around me.
It protects me as I roam
And I hang it up to dry
When I get back home.
A ragged raincoat still
Yet holds an honored place
Always there and waiting
Just for me, in case.

AS IF IT EVER WERE

I can't see the future.
Everything's a blur.
There's no apparent remedy
Or quick and easy cure.
Only one thing's certain:
Uncertainty is sure
And life will not be easy
As if it ever were.

HOME AT LAST

Thirty years ago
a younger man
stepped off of the plane.
Through all this time
the memories
of that day remain.
There were no banners
welcoming,
no crowds to call his name,
but what he thought was his
was instead his nation's shame.
He swallowed all the pain
for that's what a hero does
but now it's time
to recognize
this man for who he was:
A soldier on a mission
who served his nation's call
for we owe a mighty debt
to him
and his companions all,
the ones whose names
are here inscribed
upon the solemn stone
and the ones
who run their fingers
over names
they once had known.
It's hard for him to think
that so much time has passed
yet it feels so good
to hear those words,

"WELCOME HOME AT LAST!"

Written for the Vietnam Veterans' Homecoming at Branson, Missouri
in the early 2000's.

HEART OF A NATION

Deep within her bosom
the heart of a nation beats
from country roads and rivers
to the noise of city streets.
From her wheat-filled plains
to the paddies of the 'heel
Missouri is America
where dreams transform to real.
From the hills and hollows
we can hear her song.
Beautiful and boisterous!
Humble, and yet strong!
Nations rise and flourish
from the vigor in their hearts
and America is blessed
that Missouri's where it starts.
It flows as mighty rivers
from this blessed land
endowing me as well
for Missouri's where I stand.
Here I'll make my home
where my own heart has found
a wholesomeness of spirit
in Missouri's hallowed ground.

Missouri has become our home.

THE ONLY STALLION

There is one stallion standing
At the far end of the field
And I wonder by his stature
What secrets are revealed.
What is so audacious
In setting self apart?
Does it signal someone
Examining his heart?
Is this the only stallion
To wander all alone
Or am I as much a target
For thinking on my own?
Perhaps the stallion scares
The remainder of the herd.
Is that the reason for
The rancor I've incurred?
He is a noble figure
As he shakes his glossy mane
And seems to know his freedom
Is contentious to maintain.
He's a target for his solitude
As he snorts and paws the earth,
A reminder of what freedom costs
And also what it's worth.

STONE PILLARS

Stone pillars on a vacant lot,
A house and home that time forgot,
Alone now on this empty space
I must now my failure face:
Expectations far too great,
A young man fallen from their weight.
An older man with weary eyes
Looks for help from distant skies.
The young man called, it never came.
The old man fears the very same.
With fading hope he draws each breath

And looks afar beyond his death.
With words he travels - quick - through time.
To the stars he seeks to climb.
The old man feared the young man dead
But lived in long lost dreams instead.
The expectations are long past
But he fulfills them now, at last.

SWANS IN SUNLIGHT AND SHADE

Through the central window pane
and framed by leaves of green
two swans swim together
not knowing they've been seen.
Beautiful and graceful
they seem to be divine
and drawing close together
somehow intertwine.
Two becoming one
greater than the parts,
on this day we celebrate
the joining of our hearts.
And like the swans in sunlight
that glide on ponds of blue
you see only me,
and I see only you.
And though the sunlight settles
and passes into shade
the scene outside my window,
like our love, will never fade.

I saw the two swans on Mirror Lake at Grant's Farm
as I ate lunch in the breakroom at the General's Store nearby.

SMASHING A PENNY

I'm smashing a penny
For only two bits
And the Treasury Department
Says that gives them fits!
"It's severely depressing
The money supply!"
Which the Congress has mentioned
Is the main reason why
The Federal Reserve
Is printing some more,
Billions of dollars
So we won't be poor.
They give it to all
Except those in need.
"I'll give back the penny!"
I cry and I plead.
But it is too late!
The economy's crashed
And it's all because
Of the penny I smashed.

Some thoughts from the depths of the Great Recession
as I sat beside the penny smashing machine at Grant's Farm.

THE CHUBBY DINOSAUR

I saw a chubby dinosaur
at the Federal Reserve today
talking to the chairman.
Here's what I heard them say.
"Quantitative Eating!" said the dinosaur.
"Awesome! I need a lot more chow!"
"Not eating! EASING! You stupid dino -
Everybody run! NOW! NOW! NOW!!!"

Chubby was introduced in *The Dinosaur's Lingerie* in 2014.
Look for LOTS more "Chubby Dinosaur" poems in
The Chubby Dinosaur: Some poetry bites coming soon!

THE WISE OLD CAMEL

The wise old camel
cocked its head at me.
"What makes you think," it asked,
"I give advice for free?"
"I don't know," I said,
"Would you like another task?
A camel must obey me
and do just what I ask."
"Feed me first", it said,
"and your request will be discussed
in a friendly atmosphere
once we've built some trust."
I got a pail of grain
and the camel commenced to eating
but afterwards refused
to go on with our meeting.
It said it didn't like
my surly attitude
and that I crossed the yellow line
between impolite and rude.
It hasn't said a single word
to anyone since then
although it sometimes winks at me
and gives a knowing grin.
"Outsmarted by a camel!"
I know that's what you're thinking
but I fathom its suggestion
and accept it without blinking.
For if a camel deigns
to give me manners cues
mine must be pretty bad
so what've I got to lose?

THE ENGLISHMAN'S UMBRELLA

The Englishman's umbrella
Is more cherished than a jewel
And he refuses to unfurl it
As if it were a tool.
It gives a sense of style
And swagger to his stroll
For conveying rank and class
Is his greater goal.
In London exhibitions
Of rain occur a lot
But umbrellas opened up
And common sense do not.
The Englishman would rather
End up getting wetter
Saving his umbrella
For a day when weather's better.
Yes, there's a certain brashness
That I cannot explain
As the English muster on
And just ignore the rain.

THE AMERICAN'S UMBRELLA

There are twenty in the basement
And behind the closet door,
Five inside the car.
In the trunk there may be more.
Everywhere I look
Another one is found
Until the first of raindrops
Hits the barren ground.
"Where is my umbrella?"
I hear a thousand roar
And all get soaked transitioning
From car into the store.
The Chinese-made umbrellas
Sell thirteen bucks a pop
And American indebtedness

Unlike the rain won't stop
Until, unless, amazingly,
We find all those umbrellas
And with the deficit in trillions,
Let's start lookin', fellas!

HOG HOLLOW HEAVEN

I saw a hog a-wandering
By the riverside
And the fun it had in the mud
Making its own slide.
I saw it run in circles
Like a carousel
And later find a quiet place
And lie down for a spell.
I would say that it was sleeping
For as it lay there by the stream
I saw it stir and smile
As if in a happy dream.
I cannot say what brought it here
Or why this place it chose
But it takes hog hollow heaven
Everywhere it goes.
It revels in the laughter
Of boys and girls like you
And their moms and dads
Who once were children, too.
Life's a mystery
With many paths to follow
And we're glad yours brought you here
To heaven in Hog's Hollow.

Written for the City of Byrnes Mill and posted on a plaque
at the park playground beside the big black and white pig!

A FIREFLY HELD

I did have a dream last night
which I forgot about
which gave me cause to contemplate
regarding the subject of doubt.
I could question the reason
for having a dream I forgot
or say there was no dream at all
as many would tell me there's not.
But I am committed and stubborn.
"I had a dream!" I insist
as the naysayers all turn their backs
which they do to all who persist.
Yet I know this, that a dream abides
for reasons all of its own
and that for my dogged belief
both my faith and power have grown.
Miracles happen around me
like fireflies flash in the night.
I may be the only one watching
to proclaim that instant of light.
For though our dreams are illusion
they are as real as a firefly held
and our hearts fill with light as our hands
when there a grand vision once dwelled.

AHEAD OF THE WOLVES

I am ahead of the wolves
and have made it – safe! – to the car
but my heart is not slowing down.
I don't how many there are.
Will they be waiting at home
ready to pounce and to bite?
What will I do if they come

in packs to attack me tonight?
My mind says to just let them take me
and hope there's not too much pain
but my body says to survive
and that to fight to live is to gain.
So unprepared am I
to wage war against such dire foes
and I fear the fear in my heart
will become the me who everyone knows.
I try to steady my hand
and with logic and reason press on
hoping and praying to see
the light that comes with the dawn.
For indeed it was only a dream.
The dangers I feared disappear
and though glad I am for the day
I'm aware that they are yet near.

A BEGINNING

I stubbed my toe on my suitcase
in the darkness last night
and I think I might have seen it
if instead of black it were white.
I'm not stupid! I just did not see it.
I take precautions to avoid a repeat
so my toe and the heavy black suitcase
do not again in such a way meet.
It's not the fault of the suitcase
and no one can blame it on me.
What it's like to be black
is something I just cannot see.
So let's not keep blaming each other
for the scrapes on our toes and our shins
for knowing you cannot know all things
is how understanding begins.

THE SOUND OF FREEDOM'S SAIL

I hear her in the cheering crowds as she marks the Fourth of July
even with the fireworks exploding in the sky.
Above the roar of crashing waves in the stiffest ocean gale,
snapping in the wind, she is freedom's billowed sail.
With open eyes I look to her, the red, the white and blue,
yet even in the darkest night her sounds keep coming through,
calling loudly,
"One and all! Never be afraid!
March beside the Stars and Stripes
in freedom's grand parade!"

With sounds of battle crashing and the din of falling shells,
through her torn and tattered weeping her agony she tells.
She cries for all her children, the noble and the brave,
who knew the cost of freedom yet for us all, they gave.
With moistened eyes I'm blinded but I can hear her still
standing guard for those who lie beneath this sacred hill,
calling softly,
"Everyone! Remember each brave soul.
To live in peace and freedom
should also be your goal."

I hear her every morning above the trumpet call
in the softly rustling breeze that touches one and all.
And she calls me in the evening as the sun begins to set.
Though taken down and folded she's not through talking yet.
I close my eyes and touch her and hold her to my chest.
Of all the flags I've ever held this one is the best,
whispering to me,
"All is well. You are safe with me.
When you hear me calling in the wind,
take heart! For you are free!"

On February 15, 2003 I heard a flag suddenly flap in the breeze
as I walked on the hill near my home. This is what it said to me.
A companion poem, "The Wind in Freedom's Sail", may be
found in my book, **Diamonds of the Dawn**.

TO THE NEWEST KNIGHTS OF CAMELOT

(Found on a parchment discovered in the ruins
and dated just before its fall.)

The Roundtable has pondered
two points of our old laws
and this epistle is to inform you
of the conclusion that it draws.
It has been decided
ideals that once were true –
be trustworthy, be loyal –
should not apply to you.
The ruling knights of Camelot
to these do not adhere
and they would only hinder you
in life it does appear.
Trusts we made with older knights
we now discard with ease
and find that we are better off
just doing as we please.
We told them, "It's to help you!"
but we all know we're lying
but when you've got the power – we do! –
why waste time denying?
Honor is a concept
to use at your own choosing
for it is better winning
by cheating more than losing.
Out with those old values!
Do not be a fool!
Get the coin and be in charge!
That's our golden rule.

A SIMPLE NIGHTMARE

I just had a nightmare
That someone stole my car
And I could never find it
Though I searched both near and far.
I woke up with a start
And went to my garage,
Saw my car and touched it.
It was no mirage!
But when I got inside
And turned the starter key
The engine didn't roar.
It only clicked at me.
I went to kick a tire
But all of them were flat
And realized there was no one
Who'd steal a car like that!
I cried out in frustration
And struggled back to bed
And as I lay there writhing
This thought went through my head:
I took a simple nightmare
And somehow made it worse
And as I watch the news right now
I think that's mankind's curse.

BOYS AND LLAMAS

I have just discovered
why llamas are a hit.
Boys especially like them
because of how they spit.
I guess they think it's cool
that the females of that clan
can hock a loogie just as well
as any male or man.

HOPPING FOR A STAR

I saw a kangaroo
Last night in a dream
Hopping high to catch
A twinkling starlight beam.
It could never reach it
However high it hopped
But the kangaroo in my dreams
Never ever stopped.
Oh, it might have paused a bit
Every now and then
To ponder new approaches,
Rest and start again.
And when my dreams like starlight beams
Seem a bit or way too high
I remember how the kangaroo
Would always ever try.
So if sometime in future years
You hear I tried and failed
Know this: That in my heart
I will have prevailed.
So before you dismiss and ridicule
Those silly dreams of ours
Remember that old kangaroo
That hopped to reach the stars.

A HORSE TO BE MY FRIEND

A horse can only take me thirty miles a day
and my destination is seventy away.
My car can get me there quickly in an hour
excepting for its battery has just now lost its power.
And thus I must upon my own two legs depend

and suddenly I wish I had
a horse to be my friend.

ENDS WITH "MOO!"

Shakespeare never ended
a poem with the word.
I think he must have thought
that it was too absurd.
They never ever taught it
when I went to school
but next to "Kiss a Llama!"
it's the most important rule.
Why is it they teach us how
to line up quietly
and then that we should blind ourselves
to things we ought to see?
Can you teach imagination?
I'm not sure you can
but its presence is inherent
in the heart of every man.
We try so hard to block it
but it is like the tide,
too powerful to keep
forever locked inside.
And now mine has escaped
as cows can sometimes do
and I don't care what they say!
This poem ends with "MOO!"

MULES IN MISSOURI

I have a stubborn mule
that hasn't got a clue!
It won't pull my plow
like the horses do.
I push and pull and push and pull
but its feet are stuck like glue
and it's a very stupid mule
'casue it keeps saying,

"MOO!"

THE CAT AND THE CANDLE

She watches the candle
as it flickers and twists
almost as if
it is all that exists.
And in her eyes the candle
reflects its orange flame
mimicked by her tail
as if it were all a game.
And yet with such intensity
does the feline stare
that she does not even notice
my sitting in the chair.
She will watch all night
until the flame has died.
Her patience and her purring say
she feels good inside.
Is it curiosity
or is my cat on guard?
Either way I've come
to hold her in regard.
For distracted not by circumstance
nor howling of the wind
she keeps her eyes upon her task
and sees it to the end.

THE KITTEN AND THE PUMPKIN

The kitten was amazed
At the flickering it saw
In the pumpkin's mouth
So it stuck in its paw.
I feared its curiosity
Would be a painful flaw
But it knocked out the flame
With the quickness of its draw.
I marvel at the kitten
That risks such lethal law
And for its luck and recklessness
I stand open-mouthed in awe!

FOR ITS REMAINING

They leveled the hill
on which the house stood.
Gone were the monuments
of his childhood for good
save for the tree
whose shade he knew well
and for its existence
he has stories to tell.
A little boy laughing
with puppy in tow,
for the tree's isolation
it's a story I know.
Brothers who threw
a ball with their dad,
his one earnest wish
was to make them all glad.
And a mother whose love
poured out from her hands
for food is a nurture
a boy understands.
The house where she cooked
and sewed is long gone
as is the family
who sat on its lawn.
Only the tree
is left to attest
yet for its remaining
all who know it are blessed.
The life of a person
is about picking and choosing
the things that last longer
than winning or losing
which like the tree stand
strong and alone.
Had it not been for loss
I would never have known.

IVAN THE TERRIER
AND THE AUTUMN LEAVES

He chases after leaves
that crinkle in his teeth
though each one is big enough
for him to hide beneath.
He treats them as if prey!
As a tiny wolf he plays.
Ivan makes me laugh
in - Oh! - so many ways!
I think it must be instinct,
the way his brain is wired,
for he would fetch each single leaf!
But now he's getting tired.
He's just a tiny little dog
on such a giant planet.
A silly dog that chases leaves
can't change a thing!

Or can it?

His determination
to gather every leaf
cannot be achieved
yet it causes him no grief.
He rests when he is tired,
panting in the sun,
confident that in the end
he will somehow have won.
He's in a battle he can't win
yet he will not concede
and for his courage he has changed
this man's life, indeed.

MY TWO GOAT GIRL

I fell in love with a two-goat girl
When I had exactly none
And I was told there was no way
Her heart could e'er be won.
But there she stood before me
As gorgeous as could be
And my heart said that two measly goats
Were not too much for me.
I signed on with a pirate ship
and sailed the ocean wide
And though it earned me just one goat
I would not be denied.
I climbed the tallest mountain
In search of gold and fame,
Bought myself a second goat
And went home to make my claim.
Looking somewhat older
And quite a bit more weathered
It was with great confidence
I walked with two goats tethered.
I sauntered up the path
And upon her door I knocked.
Her father answered, saw the goats,
And looked a little shocked.
"I'm here to date your daughter," said I.
"I've brought two goats with me."
He blinked and gulped and then he growled,
"For you, the price is three!"
But I decided then and there
His demands were much too much
'Cause a two-goat man is far too proud
To ever stand for such.
She ran away with me that night!
For her, two goats were fine
And I'm a wealthy man today
'Cause now we're up to nine!
She'll always be my two-goat girl
and for that I am so glad
But please don't pass on our address
To her three-goat dad!

LIFE AT A CANTER

I see a horse at a canter
neither racing or stretching in strife
and wonder why I can't move
with such grace as I journey through life.
For all has been gallop and go
for as far back as I can recall
and I don't remember a canter
across the meadow at all.
Everything's competition.
Living is all about winning
but here at the end of my life
I'm seeking a brand-new beginning.
No one wants an old racehorse
who dreams of life at a canter
and imagines life could be better
with luxuries thinner and scanter.
And I don't care to be wanted.
What they want I've given and more.
The life I'll live at a canter
will be better than ever before.
For I see the spark in the eyes
of the horse as it canters and dances
gleefully blending with time
that it like a lover romances.

This is how I felt as I approached retirement
and how I feel now!

ONE MORE MOUNTAIN

One more mountain lies ahead
taller than the rest
and I wonder if I have enough
to pass this hardest test.
I have traveled many miles
on this toilsome trail
surprising others and myself
who were certain I would fail.
Could it be that they were right
and I don't have enough?
I know the pain that lies ahead
though my muscles have grown tough.
So I raise my eyes and look beyond
the mountain standing tall
sure that I'll succeed
when I commit my all.
I do not know what obstacles
I will yet endure
yet start to climb the mountain
the final outcome sure.

WRECKED BY A WEED

I think of myself as an over achiever
But that was before I met cedar fever.
It's more than an allergy. It's an all out attack
Which has for three days had me flat on my back.
My feet are not running but my nose sure has been
And I'll wait 'til April e're I come here again.
I'm finally doing what my momma said do
And hoping the cedars don't do this to you.
I'm staying inside and showering off.
I gargle with saline to temper my cough.
"Welcome to Austin!" the airport signs beckon
And I'll take home a lesson from this visit I reckon.
" Go not to Texas when the cedar's in seed
Lest the best of your plans get wrecked by a weed!"

WALKING ON EDGES

When I was younger
I walked on the edges
of logs fallen over
across distant ledges
and in the adventure
of youth unafraid
the frame of the person
of today was thus made
and through the defeats
of which scars are a token
came a quieter man
with spirit unbroken.
Still taking chances
with impossible odds
on the edges of fate
what's left of me trods,
the part and the parcel
of the boy I once knew
who carries the faith
that he never outgrew.

ONE GREEN PUNCHBALL

One green punchball
against a sea of red
so instead of crimson
I remember green instead.
For even though it's tiny
it offers evidence
that daring to be different
defies insignificance.
But it's just a stupid punchball
and I'm a silly poet
yet gave you seed for thought
in hopes that you might grow it.

IVAN THE TERRIER AND THE STARS

I would never see a star
Save for that small dog
Nor the sun arise to melt
The early morning fog.
I would never walk around
The house as I now do
Since Ivan wanders anyplace
His nostrils tell him to.
And should I see a star at night
Though far from home I be
I always think of Ivan
And know he thinks of me.
And isn't there a joy in that,
To love and be loved back?
The stars in Ivan's eyes say,
"Of my love there is no lack!"
He's just a silly little dog
Who barks at cats and cars
And yet a gift from heaven's heights
To tend me towards the stars.

HOW FAR A SMILE?

How much money will I have
Once all the bills are paid?
This is a question sobering
And how a budget's made.
But I who am a poet
Keep a ledger different kind,
One that measures only if
I reach the heart and mind.
And yesterday I got
A return from years ago.
A young man smiled at me!
"It's your llama book I know!
My mom and dad bought it here
when I was only two.
We read it every night back then
And, sometimes, we still do!"
And I wonder at the mettle

Of the younger man I was
And look into this old man's eyes.
Does he still have it? Yes, he does!
How far a smile can travel!
How long a laugh can last!
How quickly we grow up and old!
Life goes by so fast!
And yet inside a yellow book
A little boy once carried
Love extended long ago,
Priceless now, has tarried.

From a conversation in Branson, Missouri, in March 2017.

THE RARE ONE

It is the rare one
who is truly bold and brave
who calculates not the odds
in his bid to save.
It is the rare one
who gains his heart by giving
and changes for the better
the life that he is living.
It is he who wanders
with eyes to tend above
acknowledging the blessings
of a Greater Love.
It is rare to find someone
who is truly free
yet there the one I taught
is now teaching me.
See how he advances
where others choose to yield!
It is through such action
the rare one is revealed.
And it has been my honor
to stride with one so rare
and should he in need but whisper
in that instant I'll be there.

For Ryan.

ALPHABETICAL LIST OF POEMS